ADVANCE PRAISE FOR VERMONT MOMENTS:

A must-have book for anyone who wants to know the real
Vermont. Dick Drysdale's Vermont exists today in the tiny
towns, schools and churches still scattered in every county in
the state. Whether we live in Burlington, Rutland, or Brattle-
boro, Dick's version of Vermont explains why we are who we
are. We are cheerful, industrious, practical, frugal and generous at the same time, tolerant, and community minded. And
we are so because our ancestors who lived in small Vermont
towns, long ago and more recently, taught us to be so.

—Howard Dean, Vt. Governor, 1991-2003

Some of the finest writing anywhere on the evanescence of
Vermont's sense of rural community. Drysdale's articles tran-
scend conventional journalism and leave us with an array of
poetically crafted stories about our neighbors, towns, institutions, arts, weather, and landscapes. For anyone who ever felt
at home here, this collection will help you understand why.
For ex-pats, this superb collection may bring you home.

—Bill Schubart, author of several books,
most recently "The Lamoille Stories"

What's special about living in Vermont? Dick Drysdale has
been exploring that question for decades, and in *Vermont
Moments* he collects sixty pieces in response—random
thoughts and personal memories, salutes to fellow citizens,
the vagaries of the weather, the wilder thoughts and doings
of neighbors, and even a poem or two of surprising sureness
and delicacy. Don't be in a hurry. Read them one at a time.
When somebody wants to know what's special about living in
Vermont, give them a copy.

—Thomas Powers, of East Barnard, is a Pulitzer Prize-winning
journalist and author, whose books include "The Killing of
Crazy Horse" and "The Man Who Kept Secrets"

There are scant few who could write a book entitled *Vermont
Moments* and M. Dickey Drysdale is more qualified than any-

one else I can think of. Here are some shining moments from his contributions to *The Herald of Randolph, Vermont Life Magazine,* and *The Boston Globe,* with a few poems added for good measure. All of this bears his sensitive touch.

—*Ken Squier, owner of central Vermont's legendary radio station, WDEV, and the equally legendary Thunder Road race track*

Dick Drysdale sees with the eye of a journalist and writes with the voice of a poet. To steal a line from the author's review of "Judevine," this book stands as "a tribute to the power of truth."

—*Chris Braithwaite was publisher of The Chronicle in Barton for 40 years before selling it to his employees in 2014*

Reading Dickey Drysdale is like having fireside chats with one of your most intelligent friends. His sturdy unpretentious prose and delicate poetry transport you around Central Vermont and the world on a multi-hued literary magic carpet.

—*Bill Mares, former journalist, high school teacher and state legislator, is author or co-author of 15 books*

These stories, poems, and profiles illustrate the best of writing about real people and real places, seeing beyond the surface into an understanding of a person or place's most fundamental essence, told through the eye of the honest observer. Drysdale not only celebrates the ordinary people who make a community rich beyond words but he too is present, imbuing the pieces with his own story of belonging, of witnessing, of loving the everyday miracles that happen even when we're not looking.

—*Yvonne Daley of Rutland, Vt., author of five nonfiction books including A Mighty Storm and The Bend in the Road*

M. D. Drysdale has distilled his years as an editor into "Moments" of joy, insight, and poignant recollection. He has music in his heart, and in his poetry and his prose. *Vermont Moments* bears witness to a life well observed, well lived, and well written.

—*Marialisa Calta, a freelance writer based in Calais, Vt.*

Vermont Moments

A CELEBRATION OF PLACE, PEOPLE,
AND EVERYDAY MIRACLES

M. DICKEY DRYSDALE

Book and cover design:
Karen Thorkilsen, East Barnard, VT
www.karenthorkilsen.com

Photography:
Robert M. Eddy
First Light Studios, Randolph, VT
www.firstlightstudios.net

CreateSpace Edition

As the editor of the *Springfield Union* of Springfield, Massachusetts, he became one of New England's premier journalists. Both his daughter Eleanor, my mother, and her husband John Drysdale, my father, worked for him at the paper. To both he bequeathed his passion for journalism—and also his conviction that a newspaper should serve its community in many ways. (His premature death was due to pneumonia contracted as he delivered Christmas baskets to the homes of needy residents of Springfield, an annual charity of the *Springfield Union*.)

Maurice Dickey's principles and dedication found new birth in 1945, when John and Eleanor Drysdale moved to Randolph and purchased *The Herald* from another legendary newsman and citizen, Luther B. Johnson. They operated *The Herald* until 1973, when the job of editor and publisher fell to me. I hope that the enthusiasms and community awareness that animated my grandfather can be found in the pages of this book.

CONTENTS

FOREWORD

In his nearly 45 years as publisher of *The Herald of Randolph*, M. Dickey Drysdale has pretty much seen rural Vermont whole—the bustle of community life, the beauty of nature, the dignity of work, the exhilaration of outdoor sports, and above all, the complexity and worth of his neighbors and fellow citizens. And he has written about all of these things over the years, publishing short, evocative pieces in his weekly newspaper, along with the more standard fare of news stories, wedding notices, and obituaries.

These essays most often present the Vermont we all love and are afraid of losing. That they do so with wit and knowledge grounded by years of experience is simply an added pleasure. During my years as editor of *Vermont Life*, I was delighted to publish several of these pieces because they so accurately and evocatively convey the Vermont I know.

Vermont is more than just a "state of nature," more even than a glorious pastoral landscape. Rather, it is a place where people and nature—the land, the rivers, the mountains—have lived together, worked together, and co-evolved over several centuries.

I think of Vermont as a fabric—woven over time with stone walls and barns, villages, and fields hard-wrought from the surrounding forests. And woven also with stories, customs, artifacts, history, and folklore.

You can't explore this Vermont fabric in the abstract. You have to talk to people, walk the fields and back roads, live in one place and know its ups and downs for years to really understand it and write about it with any insight. It's a form of commitment, a commitment to place.

Dick Drysdale has lived that kind of commitment, and his essays show it. He is a master storyteller, and he seasons his stories with specific people and places—Harold Farr and Farr's Hill, the Tunbridge Fair, Tom Winship, the White River, the Chelsea Wind Harp and, memorably, his own infant son, Robin Bruce Drysdale. These and more enrich Dick's writing, and ground it in a very specific Vermont reality.

This place we love is fragile. If it is a fabric woven of time, culture, people, and the land, then if any single thread unravels, the entire fabric is weakened.

The Herald of Randolph and the essays in this book are not only a reflection of that fabric, they are part of it. Dick Drysdale's essays are evidence of its value—and one of the most positive signs that in some form, it will last.

—Tom Slayton

Tom Slayton is an award-winning journalist, author, and editor who for 21 years was editor-in-chief of Vermont Life magazine.

VERMONT MOMENTS

A Shocking Tail

I wonder how many other families have the kind of problems we are having with electric animals.

I'm not talking here about a little static from the cat's fur on a dry winter day, either. I'm talking about fully-wired electric critters, outside the house and inside the house. It's the kind of problem that, frankly, you don't expect, but you have to deal with it anyway.

For our family it all began a couple of years ago when the sheep escaped. "Escaped" is too strong a word here, because what the sheep did was merely to walk through the gate we had left open at the far end of the pasture. Nevertheless, the sheep was out, and it had to be chased.

Sheep are not much for running, but they are terrific at scampering. They'll let you craftily sidle up to within ten feet of them, as a panic-stricken look builds in their luminous eyes, and their ears start doing a little semaphore act atop their heads. Suddenly, the panic boils over into action in all four legs at once and zip—they're gone. You trudge after them again.

This particular sheep led me by degrees to a nearby farm, when it got into a thick stand of wet weeds and poor footing that made it stumble. It was cornered, and I flung myself atop the poor creature and pinned it, kicking wildly, to the ground. I was not prepared for what happened next.

ZAP! A jolt crashed through my body as I held the sheep. Then, ZAP, another one. Trying numbly to think through the situation, I could come to only one conclusion: I had tackled an electric sheep!

I almost let go, but when the third surge set my teeth to grinding, a pattern began to emerge. One surge every second. Hmm. I looked around carefully and sure enough, snaking through the wet weeds I spied the gleam of a wire—an electric fence. ZAP! It took me just one more second—and one more blast from the fencer— to get that sheep off the ground, reacting with a pump of animal adrenaline like the ones that had kept the sheep one step ahead of me.

We all got the poor terrified thing back in the pasture, and after awhile, I felt more sorry for the sheep than for myself. That sheep had had a pretty bad day.

Not as bad a day, however, as was experienced by the rat in the kitchen last summer. I don't actually know how the rat had gotten trapped at the top of the gas stove. I just know that one night my wife and I said goodbye to a few friends and went to tend to the dishes—and there the critter was.

We wondered if the guests had seen it but were too polite to say so. In truth, it was hard to miss: a full-grown rat with its rump, tail and splayed back legs plastered against the blue-and-white tiles on the wall of the kitchen, just about eye level. It had gotten trapped by the stove, which had apparently been shoved to the wall just as the rat nosed into the wrong place at the wrong time. You could say it was schmushed. It was certainly dead.

Still, you don't want to just grab a rat. I used kitchen tongs, metal ones. Bad choice.

I carefully targeted the deceased rat's tail and squeezed the tongs. ZAP! The familiar current raced up my arm as I dropped the tongs and jumped back in pain and astonishment. Damn! An electric rat this time!

As it turned out, the rat, though trapped against the wall by the stove, had had time for one desperate act. Defiantly, it sank its teeth into the nearest thing at hand—which turned out to be the electric cord. Mr. Rat never moved again. And he never released the 110-volt wire from the clamp of his teeth, remaining in death a kind of organic jumper cable, waiting for someone to clamp onto the other end.

The someone turned out to be me.

The electric sheep turned out to be OK.

The electric stove was inoperable for a week.

We still pat the dog, but we wear rubber gloves.

LEGACY

Some hundred years ago a generous wave
Washed over these parts
Sprinkling the town
With enduring legacies—
The hospital, of course, and
Side-by-side on Main Street
The rose-hued library and the
Birch-paneled Music Hall,
Gifts of the late colonels
Kimball and Chandler

While in another neighborhood
About that same time, somebody
Decided to purchase a double lot,
One empty, grassy space
Amidst the crowd of homes.
And now every time you drive past
You smile at the happy whirl—
Girls, boys, dogs, balls, with
Sometimes a sober-faced dad
Intent on instruction;
And instead of a granite inscription,
Just a couple of well-worn
Bare spots on the lawn.

'TIL WE MEET AGAIN

East Barnard is the sort of Vermont village that you discover by accident, if at all. It's situated in the lovely rolling farmland of central Vermont, served only by three gravel roads. All of them must be traversed for at least six miles before one comes upon another settlement.

When I found it a few years back, I was lost, and the unexpected pleasure of finding myself in East Barnard stayed with me. Having surprised me so delightfully, the village seemed no longer a dot on the map but a charming friend.

And so when an item in *The Herald* announced that the East Barnard church would celebrate its 150th anniversary with a special service and picnic, it was as if I had been handed an engraved invitation. I accepted immediately. There's something predictably wonderful about anything having to do with anniversaries, remote Vermont villages, tiny rural churches, and picnics; putting them together seemed virtually to guarantee a poignant experience.

So it was. East Barnard is as small a collection of houses as can be fairly called a village. The half dozen or so residences cluster around the three dirt roads as they intersect. An abandoned store (not enough customers), a community building, the church, and the cemetery constitute the civic center. The church, like most of the homes, is a little standoffish, perched astride a high bank at the foot of one of the hills that rise impatiently from the brook valley. It is small, a plain white clapboard box, more an evocation of beautiful churches elsewhere than a thing of beauty itself. Mature pines, thrusting into the blue summer sky, easily overshadow the church. As elsewhere in East Barnard, man's mark is dwarfed by Nature's slate.

Down the hill, the lawn of the community building was set this day with picnic tables for the coming feast, the playground a magnet for children whose parents steered them firmly to the church. A community supper had been held the previous evening, and the remaining food had been spread on one of the tables, offered freely, 20th century manna for those who had not brought lunch of their own.

Inside the church, 200 people crowded into every pew and into chairs set against the wall. Church history was read, with wit and sympathy. Reminiscences were spoken, personal and moving. The minister, a young pastor from out of state whose ancestors had been among the town's early settlers, assured the congregation that indeed their church would last another 150 years, so long as they maintained their loyalty to the church, the community, and each other.

The choir, much expanded for the occasion, sang gloriously out of tune, the sort of spirited anthems which would have delighted the American composer Charles Ives. The congregation joined in with "Rock of Ages", "God of Our Fathers," and other hymns whose very names can bring mist to the eyes of anyone brought up in a Yankee church.

What is most moving in these anniversary occasions is the clarity of vision they present, the shared understanding about important things. For a moment the distractions of modern mores fall away, leaving a powerful affirmation of the value of community, of roots, of respected friendships, of an abiding spiritual predominance in the affairs of men.

At the end of this day's service, as people rose to go, the choir began, unexpectedly, to sing yet another favorite hymn, "God Be with Us 'til We Meet Again." The people of the congregation were already on their feet, moving toward the aisles; yet, when they heard the hymn, they were loath to leave.

What they did instead was to reach out, tentatively at first, physically, greeting old friends with a handshake or a hug. Suddenly, the room was full of people embracing and touching, emotion beaming from their eyes. Total strangers were swept up, too, and eventually the entire church-full of people, as if possessed by a common will, joined hands, singing along softly with the choir, the room bare and unpretty but awash in a beauteous spirit.

So spontaneous and ingenuous was this demonstration, so unlikely was it, considering the roomful of reserved and correct old Vermonters, that it seemed a genuine miracle had transpired. It lasted only a moment, but it was a shining moment, to illuminate the rest of the day.

MAHATMA

Gandhi, it is said, used to lie naked
But abstemious
With the cousin he would have loved
But that he cared more for
The delights of a disciplined soul.

Here in Vermont
Our tri-color cat lies atop
The backrest of the oaken Morris chair
A mere three feet from the window
And the feeder beyond where feathered morsels
Swoop gaily to their feast, while she
Betrays not the slightest predatory interest,
Splayed out on the cushion,
The very picture
Of Enlightenment.

Requiem for a Lost Childhood

*Published in The White River Valley Herald
on December 11, 1986; reprinted in Vermont Life*

Harold J. Farr, whom *The Herald* once called "the father, grandfather, and great-grandfather of skiing in Randolph," died early Tuesday morning at the Tranquility Nursing Home, where he had been the last few months. He was 90.

For 50 years, Farr ran a dairy farm on Elm Street, now the residence of the John Palmer family. In the summer his cows grazed on the steep and scenic hill which runs up to Randolph's north reservoir.

But in the winter, the cows went into the barn, the fences came down, and Farr's farm was transformed into Farr's Hill, a magic place of thrills and spills for two generations of Randolph children.

It just so happened that the east-facing slope of the hill, the length, breadth, and steepness of it, made it an ideal ski slope, small enough to be served by a small rope tow yet precipitous enough to daunt any but the most daring.

And it just so happened that Harold Farr loved having kids around, loved seeing them active and learning, and cared not a whit for his own time and expense.

As a result, Farr operated for 30 years an extraordinary community resource—a ski hill which was open to everyone, every weekend and during school vacation weeks—all for free. Adults sometimes dropped a contribution in the box—a quarter, maybe—but for the children it was absolutely free.

Dates are a little indistinct, but it is believed that Farr started his legendary ski lift in 1936—only two years after the first ski lift in North America opened in Woodstock. He ran it until Pinnacle Ski-Ways opened in 1966. In gratitude, Pinnacle named its practice slope after him.

The ski slope was not Harold Farr's first offering to neighborhood children. For 10 years, a big skating rink was flooded next to the Farr home, and children from all over trouped to it on winter afternoons.

Farr also built a hair-raising toboggan chute all the way from the reservoir past his barn, filling in with rough rock construction where necessary. Toboggans came off that hill so fast, remembers Bob Race, that "we could jump all the way over Elm Street."

Yet it was the skiing that lingers in the memories of hundreds of former youngsters. Farr drove the tow—about 500 feet long, with a vertical drop of maybe 200 feet—from a gasoline motor housed in a little shed attached to his barn. A skiing day would find him at the engine controls, ready to stop the lift in a moment if necessary, his face uplifted as he watched the upward progress of the skiers—no more than three on the rope, please. Or his twinkly eyes would survey the line of maybe 25 kids shouldering and edging each other in line in a perpetual mini-drama to see who could get through the line most quickly.

All day long he would stand there, almost motionless, from early morning until it was too dark for safety. In the snow with his rubber barn boots, visored hat, and weather-beaten denim jacket all day—all day during the sunny springlike days and all day, too, during the blustery northers when the kids turned blue with the cold.

The kids didn't think it was unusual for a man to stand there all day and run his creaky engine on his own pasture with his own rope and his own gasoline so that they could learn to ski. The kids thought that that was the usual way of the world.

They know now how wrong they were.

Some days, the gas engine would have problems, and then Mr. Farr would hitch up the rope directly to the power drive of his farm tractor. The kids were in favor of this, because the tractor could move more kids more quickly to the top of the hill. And when he had a rope-full of big, strong skiers, Mr. Farr would touch the accelerator a little, and his eyes would twinkle even more as the youngsters sped upwards, exulting.

TWO WAYS DOWN

Once you got up to the top of Farr's Hill, there were generally two ways down. If you were big and brave, you started directly down, on the steepest part of the hill, gingerly watching for the spots where the ice usually built up and turning carefully until you dared take a straight run to the bottom. If you were younger, you took a track southward, along the top of the hill, trotted out your newly-learned snow-plow turn, ever so slowly and carefully, and headed back on a diagonal to the main part of the hill. Specifically, you headed toward the enormous elm perched a third of the way up the hill. Once you were there, it was easy coasting.

(My mother skied Farr's Hill only once. Not knowing any better, she pointed her skies over the top and skied straight down, without a turn. She survived.)

There were other ways down, of course, for the experts to ply. There were The Ledges, a rocky, gully-ridden jumble on the north side of the rope which you could ski if you could make two quick turns, in exactly the right place, and ride out the bumps with your knees.

Making The Ledges ski-able, of course, required Mr. Farr to cut his fences in a couple more places. The fences were cut.

And there was the ultimate challenge: straight down, right beside the tow, with a jump in the middle. Only a guy named Peachy Monroe could handle that, and his name still lives in memory for that feat, although unaccompanied by any other biographical notation.

During many of the years that Harold Farr operated his ski tow, lessons were given by the late Eben Brown of South Royalton. Between "Brownie" and Farr's Hill, Randolph youngsters found themselves well prepared when they ventured out onto the more altitudinous slopes at Mad River Glen or Stowe.

In a nod to the steepness of Farr's Hill, Brownie told his young charges that if they could ski from top to bottom under control, they could negotiate any ski run in the state. His students found him to be correct.

For 30 years, the winter weekends of many Randolph youngsters were spent on that hill, or trying to bump each other off the rope by thumping it with an elbow, or huddling into the tiny corrugated iron warming hut where a cast iron stove could burn your mittens brown if they touched it.

Born in the infancy of downhill skiing, Farr's Hill occupied a space in time that seems infinitely removed from today's $30 lift tickets, million-dollar damage suits, ski areas that are really land developments, and natty ski outfits.

The passing of Farr's Hill came in 1966; its successor, Pinnacle Ski-Ways, closed 10 years later in 1976. The big elm in the middle of the ski slope died last year and casts a skeletal shadow over the hill. Eben Brown died last October 4. Mr. Farr himself died Tuesday. It is not easy to be consoled.

GO ANYWAY

You've planned the hike for a month. It's the only free Saturday in sight, and for weeks, the mountains have been beckoning.

But this Saturday morning is not as you had imagined it. Clouds hang low, the wind is a little raw, and splatters of rain skip through the air. Your enthusiasm evaporates. Kiss the view goodbye, you think. And who needs the extra gear, and the extra worry about a cloudburst? There's plenty of yard work to do.

And yet—your muscles still ache for the trail. Part of you still wants to hike, even on this dreary day. What to do?

Over the years, I've developed a simple rule for this not-infrequent dilemma: Go. Go Anyway. Always Go Anyway.

The rule first presented itself when as a college student I determined to ski Tuckerman's Ravine for the first time. Arriving at Pinkham Notch, I found a dispiriting prospect. Temperatures hovered around 35 degrees, and a light wind whipped a freezing rain right through my poncho. Clouds cloaked the low ridges, promising that things would only get worse farther up the trail.

I was in despair. For so long I had heard of the glories of Tuckerman's—and now it appeared I was going there only to freeze, or maybe drown. It was already late afternoon, and the idea of an overnight in a Tuckerman's lean-to, wet and chilled to the bone, drained all the desire out of me.

But I went anyway. I put my misgivings behind me and climbed—just because I had nothing better to do, and I had driven specially from Boston, and I was 20 years old.

And something wonderful happened. Within a half-mile, as I climbed, the rain changed to snow—no longer penetrating with its wetness, and an adventure besides. The night in the lean-to was tolerable—and wonder of wonders, I awoke the next morning in glory. A cloudless sky hosted a bright morning sun which shone on the dramatic buttresses of the Ravine—marvels I had barely glimpsed in the clouds of my arrival.

With such an introduction, I fell helplessly and permanently in love with Tuckerman's Ravine. The skiing was terrific. And all because I went anyway.

Over the years, the rule has cropped up as consistently as bedrock on a mountain ridge. If bad weather, or an awkward schedule, intervened, I wavered. But whenever I went hiking anyway, I was glad of it. And every time I stayed home, I wished I hadn't. Slowly the rule solidified in my mind.

By now, I am an Authority. Last summer, when our family and another prepared for a short hike in the Adirondacks, the familiar warning signals arrived. Clouds. Winds. A few raindrops.

To complicate matters, we had five children under six with us, some of them courting colds. Did we really want to go out in the woods in such weather with five unhappy kids?

The closer we got to the trailhead, the more the weather threatened, and the louder grew the suggestions for a change of plans. Santa's Land wasn't far away. Maybe we could...

I smiled serenely. I had a rule, I explained.

"Go anyway," I said. "That's the rule. Always go anyway."

The rule was not particularly popular. Nor was my annoying smugness in propounding it. But we went.

Lucky for me, it didn't rain. The kids rushed off through the gloom and scampered to the top. We were even rewarded with a few rays of sunlight before descending, whooping with high spirits. I tried not to gloat.

"You see, folks, this here rule of mine...It worked, didn't it?"

But now, I must make an admission: I'm not rabid about my rule. I hike to enjoy myself, not to prove anything. I don't flirt with unsafe conditions. And if I see that a trip is guaranteed to be a disaster, I stay home. But most situations are otherwise. Usually you're playing percentages with the mountain weather. And my rule is pretty clear—if there's no actual danger, and as long as there's any chance you won't be soaked or otherwise abused by conditions, why then, give it a shot. Go anyway.

I also have to report that miracles aren't guaranteed, even with a rule to follow. Sometimes things don't get better; sometimes they get worse. But even then, even when the conditions are as bad as you feared, the rule can still come through for you, as it did for me one October on Mt. Jefferson.

I'd intended to combine business with an afternoon of pleasure, by taking a quick ascent up the Ridge of the Caps and back. Faced with fog and drizzle, however, it took a strict adherence to my rule even to get started on the trail. Once there, it became clear that, as usual in the Presidentials, the elements were growing worse as I climbed higher. Although the rain never came down hard, it never stopped, either, and the wind drove the wet into me. I did reach the summit, but only to find it sadly limited by a 20-foot view, thanks to low cloud cover. Trudging back through the relentless fog near the bottom of the trail, I had just about concluded that the day's only bonus was exercise. Then, in a golden moment, everything changed.

Somehow the sun, low in the west ahead of me, found a breach in the cloud cover and broke through. Nothing else was altered. Drizzle still fell, and the fog remained. Undaunted, the sun shined through the fog, through the droplets in the air, through the bigger drops suspended from every branch and every fern. It was as if Apollo himself had made a surprise entrance into the wet world. The very air turned a golden yellow as the rays poured into the woods, deflecting through the fog, sparkling from millions of tiny raindrop prisms. The world seemed transformed into pure light.

It was an incredible moment, a breathtaking scene, a gift of the mountains. And if I hadn't been hiking in the rain and the fog, I wouldn't have been there for the presentation. If I had done the sensible thing and stayed home, I would have missed that moment when the world changed.

But you see—I had a rule.

Go. Go anyway. It'll be fine.

How Not To Do It

Things you might not know if you never tried canoeing on the White River without quite knowing what you were doing:

1. There's a lot more water in there than you think.
2. However, there's not quite enough water to cover the rocks.
3. There are a lot more rocks in there than you think.
4. Shouting at the canoe will not make it turn to avoid the rocks.
5. Shouting at your partner will not make the canoe turn to avoid the rocks.
6. The current moves considerably more rapidly than you might think.
7. Sometimes white water indicates the presence of a rock, but sometimes it does not.
8. Sometimes the presence of a rock is indicated only by the thump on the bow of your canoe.
9. Canoe paddles can move right along downstream all by themselves.
10. When you are broadside to the river, it is very easy for the current to flow right into the canoe.
11. Canoes tip over easily.
12. The water in the White River in May is cold for swimming.
13. An overturned canoe, wedged against rock with the current flowing into it, weighs several tons.

14. Jack Kennedy over in Chelsea has a power winch that is about the only thing which will get a wedged canoe out.
15. It takes a long time to get warm and dry again.

Far More than a Concert

Reviewed on October 28, 1982
in the White River Valley Herald of Randolph

The Blanche Moyse Chorale and the Vermont Bach Festival recently brought to Hopkins Center in Hanover a complete production of the Bach B-minor Mass. The gift they gave us in so doing was inestimable.

It is not well enough understood in this state that in Blanche Moyse we have, at the height of her powers, one of the world's foremost interpreters of Bach. Nowhere in New York could one hear a more magnificent B-minor Mass, not in London, nor in Vienna from the likes of Nicholas Harnancourt.

For a moment as the Bach Festival concert began, it could have been another, less perfect evening. The first music is given to the orchestra alone, and this orchestra played well, but not perfectly. Balance and ensemble both left something to be desired.

But then the music passed to the chorus, Blanche Moyse's personal instrument, and we in the audience were privileged to enter the private musical world of a great interpreter. We were swept away by that great opening fugue subject: music which at the same time ascends and descends, possessed of both a gargantuan strength and a searing plaintiveness, reaching its greatest expression of anguish at the very moment of its greatest strength.

The 40 voices of the Blanche Moyse Chorale wrapped themselves around the music with an extraordinary unity of expression. Every entrance, every phrase was so clearly sung, so carefully conceived, so fully believed that it flew straight from the ears to the heart of the listener. The beauty of each phrase was interrelated to the next and that still to the next, so that after a full 15 minutes of music, one grand statement had emerged from the opening chorus.

From there, the concert went from strength to strength, as the orchestra quickly caught the spirit of the chorus and echoed its fervor.

Soloists, both orchestral and vocal, were superlative, sensitive both to the stylistic considerations of Bach and the emotional commitment demanded by Moyse. Indeed, on three occasions—two flute parts by the marvelous, wonderful Susan Rotholz and the final contralto solo by Lorna Myers—the emotional focus shifted briefly away from Mrs. Moyse and her chorus. Other vocal soloists were soprano Arlene Auger, tenor Seth McCoy and baritone Jan Opalach.

But the choral focus soon returned. The interpretations of the music turned a spotlight toward the words, revealing the depths of Bach's own insights. With the Angel's words, "and on earth, peace to men of good will," the music moved from a tentative hope to a joyous conviction. When the text invoked the crucifixion, the throbbing of the music became so unbearable that Christ's death, on the word *passus*, came as a relief, a moment of rest rendered by the chorus alone, as the instruments dropped out. The ensuing account of the resurrection was then so arresting, so joyful, that the listener was almost propelled from his seat.

Again, in the Sanctus, when the chorus sang the words of the Heavenly Host, it seemed as if the entire auditorium were full of angels, starting and swooping—from the chorus, then from the orchestra, and from the chorus again.

It's no real secret how Blanche Moyse has been able to turn 40 amateur singers into one of the best Bach choirs in the world. She does it through hard work—regular rehearsal on the Mass had been underway since January—and through conviction. Once she interrupted a rehearsal with a monologue on Sebastian Bach and on her life-long study of his work. She spoke of his art but also of his personal belief, and she concluded that through the greatness of that art he, far more than most men, had been able to approach the creative spirit itself. Mrs. Moyse is certain that her own communion with Bach has brought her, too, closer to that source of inspiration; and everyone in the Blanche Moyse Chorale feels the same way.

And so it is that we of the audience, through the insights, in turn, of a chorus, a committed conductor, and one of history's great artists, were privileged to partake, not only of a concert but of a great gift, a communion with the spirit of creation itself.

OLD CASSETTE

On an old cassette tape Allison Pearce
Is singing a melody from the Hebrides:
Water weaving among stones
Wan sunlight splashing over heather.

The song is just eight measures long
And when it is over
She sings it again, just the same way—
        and again, and again.
No variations needed, no embellishments
For the academic ear
Pure as a pearl moist in its shell.

If once you heard a young girl sing such a lay
As she walked a boiling shoreline, a web of fog
Spun across the marbled weft of her
        sea-green sweater,
You would want her at your side forever.

A Warm November Rain

Originally run as an editorial in The Herald.
Reprinted by Vermont Life.

We had been on the road a half-hour Sunday night, heading toward Middlebury, when it began to rain. Right away, my wife began to worry.

"One way I know that spring has come is that I'm not afraid of water any more," she said. "If my feet get wet, I'm not afraid they'll be cold for hours, and when it rains on the road, I'm not afraid it'll turn to ice."

"Not to worry," I told her. The temperature when we left Randolph had been well above freezing.

"This is a nice November rain," I told her, "only in December."

I suggested that worrying about things was a waste of time. "Unless," I challenged, "you want to turn back."

The road glistened wet as we headed north along Route 100. Somewhere between Rochester and Hancock, the car swerved.

My wife was suspicious. "Was that a skid?" she asked.

"It was a swerve," I told her. Nevertheless, I eyed the pavement with a little more respect.

The car swerved again. This time, I glanced at the speedometer and saw it bounding crazily. The speedometer does that sort of thing during a skid.

"A little greasy," I observed. My wife said nothing.

At Hancock, we turned left on the Middlebury Gap road. My wife mentioned quietly that at higher altitudes, the roads were apt to get more slippery. I explained that on a warm November-December night like this, a few hundred feet in altitude doesn't mean much.

The car swerved again. Then, suddenly, it was Disasterville.

Gone was the reassuring sparkle of rain reflected from the pavement; in its place shone a lethal dull gleam. An approaching car fishtailed in a wild arc. The road ahead was a ribbon of wet ice.

We both developed a tremendous distaste for the idea of driving to Middlebury.

"I think I'd like to turn around now," my wife ventured.

Finding a driveway, I turned around gingerly and back we crept downhill to a cozier altitude where our tires gripped the macadam surface securely again. We both heaved a sigh of relief.

As we approached Rochester, the question came up: to return the long way, via Routes 100 and 107, or the short way—over Bethel Mountain Road. I decided on the short way.

"There's not that much of a hill from this side," I explained confidently. My wife didn't say a word.

"Besides, if the temperature's dropping, the sooner we get home, the better," I added. Still silence.

Less than a mile out of Rochester, our headlights picked up that familiar deadly gleam on the pavement. The road twisted back and forth, and I had to admit it was climbing pretty steeply. A car inched down the hill toward us and we managed to miss each other.

"This is the steepest part," I remarked. "It levels off up above."

"It is also *colder* up there," my wife observed darkly. I had to admit she had a point, but there was no way I was going to drive that car down the slippery slide we had just come up.

For a change, I was right. The road did level off a bit, although still it was more of a hill than I had remembered.

"In conditions like this, you certainly learn the road in detail," I observed lightly. More silence in the car.

My wife was right, too. It *was* icier up there. We managed to negotiate, though, by keeping one wheel in the mud by the side of the road while the car sputtered and swerved.

"Quite a ditch there," I remarked, glancing hastily at the ravine three feet from the right wheel.

"I see it," my wife shot back. A tense urgency filled her voice.

Finally, we reached the end of the blacktop, a spot that marks the Bethel-Rochester line and the top of the hill.

"We made it," I sighed, and we both breathed easily once more.

Then we saw the taillights ahead: two cars, both stuck on a little hill I had forgotten about. One driver was trying to walk on the road, but his feet were slipping away from him.

We eased past the first stopped car, but the second was too far into the road, and we coasted to a reluctant halt.

"We'll just back up and turn around," I suggested. "Maybe we'll stay with friends in Rochester."

Alas, we were caught in a dip in the road, and backward turned out to be uphill as well. We were stuck, cradled in a slippery nook of Rochester Mountain 1000 feet above the warm habitations of the valley floor.

"I think we should have gone the long way," I offered generously.

⤫

Who the men were who hand-shoveled gravel from the shoulder onto the road I don't know. But their effort spared us from spending a rainy night on Rochester Mountain, and for that I thank them. The grit from those shovels was all it took to boost us the last few hundred yards to the top. With a jaunty "thank-you" on our car horn, we were off.

The trip down was easier than expected, the road slick but manageable at 10 miles an hour. Slowly, the icy sheen disappeared from the highway, and we began to relax. We let the speedometer crawl up to 20, 25, 30 miles an hour.

It was at about 30 that we hit the final, vicious spot of ice—100 yards of highway suddenly and totally glare, entirely without traction. We were in a free-fall down the road, the car delicately balanced between taking a straight course and veering into a tumultuous series of revolutions—90 degrees, 360 degrees, whatever it might take to satisfy the demon of our excessive momentum.

As my foot peppered the brake with desperate pumping strokes, I had just time to remember that we didn't even own the car.

We came out of it with a hard left and then a right, miraculously still on the road. Then the pavement was drive-able again, sparkling wet but no longer threatening.

My wife broke her silence.

"A nice November rain," she said, "only in December."

We walked the last mile home. A light drizzle still fell, freezing under our feet but striking our cheeks with a pleasant freshness. Across the valley, homes glowed softly with the warmth and light which we knew would soon reward us.

I thought of going back for our car, parked in the driveway of an understanding neighbor. There had been only one more hill when we decided to quit.

One more hill.

We continued our hike through the night air.

We had had hills enough.

November

In appreciation of David Budbill

November galloped into town today on a gale,
Slinging a vile brew
Of cold rain, snow, and
Lilliputian darts that
Sought out your face then
Danced away to the pavement.

All day,
Customers lunged through our office door
Out of the dishwater grey, gasping
With bitter recollection.

Later I stood amid swaying hulks
In the maple woods and smiled
A thank-you to you, David,
For my satisfaction
In the certainty
That it will only get
Worse.

WIND HARP ON A CHELSEA HILL

Published in the Boston Sunday Globe, July 4, 1971

In more superstitious times, it might have been
called a miracle. "The Miracle at Chelsea," the people
would have said, and the wind whispering through its
80 strings would have taken on mystic significance.
Reverent fingers would have felt the trembling of the
huge sounding box.

Perhaps an oracle would have taken up residence in
its shelter, where her words would have partaken of the
mystery of the great harp, informed somehow by the
constantly changing timbre of the wind in the strings.

Nowadays, we tend to call it a little crazy. A 20-year-
old has spent a year and a half to construct a wind harp
on a remote hill in Chelsea, Vermont, 20 miles southeast of Montpelier.

He has chipped bedrock by hand chisel, spliced 10-
inch-square oak timbers to a height of 23 feet, undertaken
massive engineering and painstaking decorative work.

He has placed his monument high in a cow pasture
almost unreachable except by foot, in a place so unpop-
ulated it is probable that few will ever visit it. He has
created something that doesn't do anything, which has
no utility, a thing of beauty which will hardly be seen.

Nevertheless Ward McCain, by his creation has
touched a source of wonder hidden within the practical
people of Chelsea. Under his gentle auspices, the towns-

people joined long-haired young people last weekend in a celebration of the construction of the wind harp.

The young people, of course, were predisposed to mystical vibrations, some of them seeming to regard the harp with almost worshipful awe. It was a treat to see them with the townsfolk sharing a meal under an apple tree in the high pasture.

It was the person of Ward McCain, creator of the wind harp, who brought them together. He fits naturally into the role of prophet—a Nordic face, rough-cropped blond hair, and gentle, direct eyes which match his warm manner.

It was the direct politeness which won over the people of Chelsea when McCain came to borrow tools to build the wind harp—that and his demonstrated ability to use and return the tools. The same qualities worked with dairy farmer Warren Mattoon, who allowed him to erect the instrument in the middle of his pasture, and who kept track of the work with fascination and did McCain many favors.

The harp was a result of a course in building instruments at Bennington College, where McCain was a student. Each class member was to build an instrument for a class project. McCain, already a sculptor who had produced two works in the Arizona desert, decided to build a monumental instrument which would utilize wind in strings.

He made a rough sketch, and the idea for the wind harp was born, taking final shape only as the work progressed. The location in Chelsea was discovered through a friend who lives in a cabin near the hill.

He assembled materials carefully. The main 10-by-10 oak timbers were bought in Maine. For the sounding box he bought California redwood and for the strings, high-tension airplane wire, the strongest made. Decor was of cast iron and more wood—including lignum vitae, chosen for its hardness; holly wood, the world's lightest color; ebony, the darkest; zebra wood, and Vermont maple.

He poured two tons of concrete for a base, chipping away bedrock by hand to dig the hole. One spliced oak timber he set vertical to a height of 23 feet and the other, rising from the same base on an angle, was made 26 feet long. From the top of the vertical timber he extended a horizontal beam, and between this and the angled timber the strings were set.

A huge sounding box, triangular in shape, he attached to the angled timber. The finishing touches included welding dozens of decorative iron plates to the top horizontal, working from a ladder, and the twisting of 80 iron coils to resemble fiddlehead ferns. Any large structural bolts were sunk into the beams and covered with inlaid wood.

McCain started the job in spring 1970, living at his friend's cabin. He tried to work through the winter, the snowiest in Vermont history, but was stopped when glue froze in his hands.

Along the way he got help from the people of Chelsea and from young friends, and he invited them to the celebration when the project was finished. Dozens of them came, driving in jeeps up a steep track or walking from farmer Mattoon's house. The farmer brought some up in a hay wagon behind his tractor.

A feast was spread out under the old apple tree just below the crown of the hill where the wind harp jutted into the sky. Visitors interrupted their meal for short pilgrimages to the instrument to listen and to feel its sounding board as any slight breeze sprang up. A huge bonfire was lit to bring the evening to a close.

And so a wind harp stands on the hill above Chelsea. Some will call it crazy, and some will wonder at it. And on a warm night, Kenny Anderson, a Chelsea boy charged by McCain with watching the harp, will bring his sleeping bag to the hill, sleep next to the wind harp, sometimes perhaps waking to the sound of its strings in the wind.

DIGGING A VERMONT HOLE

The notion that we are all in control of our own affairs has led to no end of trauma, aggression, and disappointment.

We know of no better cure for such a wrongheaded notion than to set a spade in a piece of Vermont dirt and attempt to dig a hole.

Anyone who has done weekend duty with a chainsaw in a woodlot knows for a fact that Vermont trees have already made up their minds which way the are going to fall, and woe to any woodcutter who attempts to convince them to lie down a different way.

What is less well known is that, rather like Vermont trees, Vermont holes have their own ideas of where they are going to be dug.

We had forgotten that fact about Vermont holes until we set to digging one in our lawn this weekend for a new little tree. Breaking the sod, we seemed to have found a good spot. The shovel went straight to the hilt in smooth ground.

On the second go-round, however, we were abruptly reminded about Vermont holes. The CLANG of metal on rock assaulted our ears and shuddered up the shovel into our arms. We had hit a hunk of green schist, that omni-present mineral which the Vermont legislature briefly considered, years ago, as a candidate for State Rock.

The schist protruded about four inches out into the hole we had begun and appeared to extend indefinitely into the soil beneath the lawn. So, obligingly, we moved the hole about four inches to the left. The hole had won the first round.

No sooner had we begun to dig in the new spot, however, than a duller THUD was felt: a tree root, about three inches thick, that curved gracefully along the side of our hole, pushing our shovel a little more to the left and a bit up, adding a little zig and zag to the shape of our growing hole. Not being prepared to chop up a tree root of that size, we decided that the zig-zag looked pretty good. We dug in the new direction.

So it proceeded. The hole was not actually averse to being dug—it just had very clear ideas as to what sort of a hole it was and where it should be. It nudged our shovel a little this way and then that, and we got along fine as long as we acquiesced in its wishes.

The final placement of our little tree resulted from a bit of sly subterfuge from below. Our pickaxe struck a massive piece of rock which, tantalizingly, moved a little bit, giving evidence that it might be dislodged and moved out altogether. Here was a prospect that would offer us a little bit of control over our own hole, for a change. We set to work manfully with pick and shovel until we dislodged the boulder and hauled it, about 80 pounds, onto the lawn. There it sat, and we admired this evidence of our mastery over the mute obstinacy of rock and soil.

Then we looked down into the hole.

It had moved. Its deepest point was now about a foot away from where it had last been.

Quite clearly that loose rock had been the final stratagem of the Vermont substratum to guide our spade in the direction the hole wished to be dug. When we pulled out the big rock, it left behind a pit which most assuredly had become the new hole, the place where our tree was destined to grow.

We didn't argue. We'd have looked pretty silly standing there in the light rain, arguing with a hole in the ground about a mere couple of feet left or right. We set the tree, a linden, and trusted that the young sapling would have as much patience as we in dealing with the independent-minded piece of ground that we had found for it.

YESTERDAY IN YOUR WOODS

Yesterday in your woods, Paul, that perishable trail: frail
veinous scraps of leaves
Which last October topped the tawny crests of beeches,
making an end, as we thought
Yet five months later still whole, lying lightly on the snow,
pale wraiths, less than paper,
Nested singly, cozy in a trail of depressions discovered
as they drifted,
The trail a gift of the March wind
But subtle residue as well
Of some warm pulse and purpose.
No random breeze first placed such ordered signposts, but
Perhaps a moose, bobcat, wayward collie.
Or a fox, extravagant brush pursuing tidy pawprints
For its own reason in its own time,
Followed then by the purposeless wind, the bewildered
leaves.
So follow now we Hansels on our way, for our own reasons,
Unburdened
By the mortal necessity of surprising
An unwary mouse.

"It's a Boy!"

White River Valley Herald, January 10, 1980

Not every brand new boy can wangle his way into the editorial columns of the local newspaper; but Robin Bruce Drysdale is in cahoots with the editor, and he isn't the type to allow such an opportunity to go knocking. The editor, however, is still having trouble operating the typewriter, the telephone, his shoelaces, and all the other machineries of everyday life. So if an editorial gets written at all, it will be a minor miracle.

Life to Robin Bruce, we suspect, has been four days of puzzling lights, odd thumpings and bumpings, unaccustomed drafts, troubled experiments with breathing, and the continuous clutchings of a greedy mouth toward anything within reach. Perceptions are scrambled, the universe a blur.

But just possibly, even at four days of age, Robin Bruce has sensed something else—that ever since 2:22 Sunday morning he has been surrounded by concern and love, that each cry, each yawn, palpitates hearts in a giant world far beyond his imagining. Has he any inkling that his stirrings influence—even dominate—the habits of enormous beings whose activities and purposes are hidden from him? Does he comprehend his power?

Certain it is that being born in Gifford Memorial Hospital in Randolph, Vermont gives to Robin Bruce Drysdale a start for which few could hope. Even in the hours before his arrival, he was the anxious focus of friendly, professional concern. His appearance was attended by no fewer than six grownups—a physician, a midwife, two nurses, and both parents. Each of them— and the the pediatrician who arrived minutes later— offered support, each offered judgment and expertise; each offered love.

But the six people in the birthing room of Gifford Hospital constituted only the inner ring of support. Soon, news of the eight-pound bundle that was Robin Bruce rippled outward in concentric circles, speedily outwards to more and more households. Telephone lines buzzed, bells jangled; even the services of the pulpit were engaged on his behalf. Before he was 12 hours old, Robin Bruce had 500 friends. His whole world, it seemed, had turned to take notice.

Who can explain the power of this tiny spot of warmth? How is he able thus to summon neighbors with lunch, beckon relatives from a distance, place smiles on the faces and greetings on the lips of dozens—and occasionally strike terror into the hearts of his parents?

Who knows? Certainly not Robin Bruce, whose immediate concern is how to put his entire fist into his mouth, mitten and all.

Robin Bruce may not even be aware of the love and concern which are manifest around him. But for his parents, the blessing of Robin Bruce is magnified by the joy of friends, the tangible support of community. We thank you all.

—Dick and Marjorie Drysdale

OUR OWN RAINBOW

This August was rainbow weather. No matter how bright the sunshine, the horizon always seemed to harbor a grey little cloud just waiting to scuttle across the sky, spitting raindrops into the fine air, pushing a rainbow in front of it.

About the middle of the month appeared, to many viewers in the Randolph area, one of the finest rainbows anyone had ever seen, with all the colors distinct, shining equally bright from the zenith down to the ground on both sides. This particular rainbow occasioned quite an amount of comment and speculation. It may have been the same phenomenon that sparked naturalist Gale Lawrence's observations, which appear elsewhere in this issue of *The Herald*.

The question inevitably arose—how many rainbows were there? Our neighbors down the road came outside when we did, and looked in the same direction; it was generally agreed that we saw the "same" rainbow. Other people around Randolph saw rainbows at that same time—but was it the same one?

Our rainbow seemed to lie only about a half-mile away, with each end securely implanted in Kermit LaBounty's pastureland. On the other hand, people in Randolph Center, four miles to the east, saw a brilliant rainbow at exactly the same time—but they saw it while looking east, not west toward ours. It must have been, we all agreed, a different rainbow, but perhaps one from the same family.

The truth about rainbows, as pointed out in Gale Lawrence's column, is that the exact position of the rainbow depends on the position of the sun in the sky and the position of the viewer. Because the rainbow is actually a spectrum of light reflected by raindrops back to one spot, a group of people looking at a rainbow are actually seeing several rainbows, no matter how close they are to each other. A man in one spot sees a different set of raindrop reflections than does his wife just 10 feet away.

The fact is, and there's some poetry involved, that we each have our own rainbow. Others may see a rainbow, too, but ours is ours and theirs is theirs. And the pot of gold at the end of our rainbow is not the pot of gold at the end of our neighbor's, nor is our land of dreams "over the rainbow" quite the same as his.

There's comfort in the undeniable, scientific fact that amidst the enormity and variety of creation, someone has seen to it that we each get our own rainbow.

FLOATING OVER CENTRAL VERMONT

As Wendy Higginson finished the breakfast dishes at her comfortable South Barnard home, gazing out the window at the sparkling October foliage, her nanny goat shot around the corner of the house in a panic. At the same time, she heard the pounding hooves of her two horses, apparently in stampede.

Suddenly, a terrific roar filled the air, and Wendy detected crackling in the branches of her apple tree, just 50 feet away. Worst of all, a giant shade passed over the morning sun, abruptly cutting off the light that seconds before had been streaming into her kitchen.

"My Lord," Wendy said to herself. "My day has come."

But the panic, like the shadow over the sun, passed quickly. A second look revealed a giant hot air balloon coasting in serenely for a landing. It was only Ken Marchuk's way of dropping in for an unexpected visit.

Ken Marchuk is the complete balloonist. Not only does he provide hot air balloon rides over Central Vermont, but his company, The Cliff Hanger, sells, insures, and services balloons and teaches the course required for certification of balloon pilots. He even sponsors festivals for hot air balloons, colorful extravaganzas in which dozens of skyships float along valleys and over the hills to test their speed and accuracy of navigation.

The balloon trip which ended in Wendy Higginson's back yard began at the White River Valley Campground, a narrow spit of land where most of the village of

Gaysville nestled before the 1927 Flood swept it away. The balloonist had invited this writer and a friend to meet at 7 AM to see the spectacle of a Vermont autumn from a unique vantage point.

The morning dawned without a whisper of wind, the light blue of morning sky unblemished by clouds. The trip had been arranged weeks in advance, but by luck we had picked the absolute peak of the foliage season, when the trees practically leapt from the hillsides, shouting with color.

Marchuk admitted it looked like a perfect day, but nevertheless he worried about predictions of a stiff breeze later on. The wind is the greatest adversary in hot air ballooning, and Marchuk prefers not to fly in winds of more than 10 miles an hour.

At the campground we had our first look at The Mighty Quinn, a 300-pound expanse of brightly colored ripstop nylon, holding 80,000 cubic feet of air which can lift a 705-pound payload. The snug basket, made of heavy-duty wicker, was just large enough for three passengers and three cartridges of propane to keep the hot air hot.

The nylon unfolded endlessly until it covered almost half of the intimate launching meadow, while most of the campground's guests slumbered unsuspectingly. A motor-driven fan was cranked to life and blew a minor hurricane of cold air into the balloon mouth until the nylon billowed and began to take on a flabby semblance of its eventual shape. Then Marchuk ignited the propane burner and a massive flame shot into the opening, warming the air trapped inside until it became lighter than the morning chill outside.

Slowly, the laws of nature began their work, and the great envelope roused itself from the grass and stretched toward the sky. Softly, magically, 1000 pounds of nylon, basket, and passengers rose up and over the treetops. Upturned faces receded, and the White River became a blue cord of water, dotted with white rapids.

Marchuk guaranteed we would fly to Randolph, 12 miles away, and in fact the balloon started in the right direction, following the narrow valley northeast from Gaysville. But as soon as the balloon reached a greater altitude, the breeze changed direction, and we headed south.

"I usually guarantee very loosely," Marchuk advised. He gave the balloon a shot of propane which lifted us about 1300 feet above the valley floor. He was hoping to find enough wind to propel us beyond the wooded wilderness which lies on the ridge between Gaysville and Barnard, our new goal.

The woods spread a carpet directly below our feet, but the balloon was in no hurry to go anywhere. We wondered, a little anxiously, what would happen were we to run out of wind above a forested area.

No problem, Marchuk assured us. Treetop landings are part of every pilot's course of instruction, he said. He had landed in trees four times in as many years, he added lightly. You just settle in gently, he explained, parting the branches as you go down, until you reach a stable limb, and then you stop.

Everything considered, we were glad to see the wind pick up a little.

The view was stunning. With the White River orienting our gaze, we peered over ridge after ridge of flaming autumn foliage southwest to Pico and Killington, southeast to Ascutney, east to Moosilauke, and west to the spine of the Green Mountains.

In the foreground rose the gentler hills which are Vermont's true glory, half-mountains scattered everywhere in a dazzling array of shapes and sizes, some aligned neatly in ridges, others poking up stubbornly at random, as though defying any attempt to order them. And swarming over everything was the magnificent forest of maples, beeches, and birches, each decked out in the favored party attire of its species. Only the scattered clumps of evergreen stood somberly, as if taken aback by all the festivity.

Directly below, dirt roads explored intimate little valleys we never knew existed, serving isolated farms and homes. At a discreet distance to the west floated our own plump shadow, a dark blimp coasting through the reds, oranges, and yellows. Since our craft moved at the speed of airstream, it seemed to us as if the wind had stood still.

Our reverie was broken as our pilot, pondering the direction our balloon was taking up a narrow valley, was heard to mutter, "Now how am I going to get out of here?"

Navigation, we concluded, is an imperfect art. However, the balloonist does have some control, because winds at different altitudes blow in different directions. The pilot gauges ground wind direction by watching chimney smoke, and he lifts or lowers the balloon to change direction. Added control is created by flaps which can be operated by the pilot to speed a descent.

Like every vehicle, the balloon can be equipped with accessories, and Marchuk usually carries an altimeter, a variometer to show the rate of ascent or descent, and a digital pyrometer, which tells the temperature of the air in the bag.

After we cleared the ridge, air speed picked up a little—to about six or seven knots, Marchuk estimated. We passed Barnard to the southeast, the miniaturized village clustered around Silver Lake, a four-color postcard.

On occasion the door of a farmhouse flew open and out popped adults, children, and dogs, all craning their heads upwards, alerted by the sound of a propane burst. Livestock bolted across a brook. Two lads grabbed their bicycles, and trailed us as long as the valley road and the wind above were of similar mind.

We poked along a couple of miles west of Route 12, heading toward Woodstock, but our slow start made it apparent that we wouldn't get there. With the fuel about half gone and the ground wind quickening, Marchuk began looking for likely fields in which to land. He spied two, about half mile ahead, shaped like runways for the approaching airship.

Choosing one of the runways, Marchuk began his descent. Suddenly, we became acutely aware that the landing field included a farm pond of generous dimension toward which we were heading. We were also aiming right at Wendy Higginson's apple tree.

Marchuk applied a little propane, and we lifted enough so that we merely glanced off the top of the apple tree, the twigs sweeping noisily along the wicker basket. Below, a white goat and two horses started at the roar of propane and ran off in three directions.

Briefly, Wendy Higginson thought her world was coming to an end.

"Oh rats," said Marchuk, or something to that effect. The words were not comforting. The farm pond was dead ahead.

Summoning all his expertise, the balloonist applied a final burst of propane. That was enough for us to clear the water and– barely–the dike beyond. The basket bounced once on the edge of the dike, throwing us a little into the air. Down we came again, and this time the slope was steep enough to capsize the basket, passengers and all, so that the landing lacked something of the dignity of the launch.

Suddenly, buildings, trees, and hills assumed their usual perspective. John and Wendy Higginson came running to help, and our balloon ride was over. But it will be a long time before we forget the intoxication of that bright October morning we spent floating over a flaming countryside.

MIDDLE OF THE DAMN ROAD

Dead in the middle
Of Mason Road just past Milt's place,
These three young guys had
Stopped their old rattletrap and were
Clambering all over each other to get
A better view up at the hillside.
No amount of agitation on my part
Could distract their gaze back
To the road that had been
Taking me to lunch.
When finally they got underway again
They flashed huge grins,
In jubilant apology.

It was only a deer,
In crisp profile against yesterday's snow.

That crew, I'd guess, were mostly
Thinking venison, but seeing
The warm pulse of life against the
Still hillside
And the gentle flow of the doe's neck
From her shoulders downward
To the browse at her feet, I too
Pulled my car to a halt.

Lunch could wait
On this blessing.
Wait on this grace.

JIM HUTCHINSON

Jim Hutchinson was a big-hearted guy.

Jim was big in a lot of ways. His presence filled a room. He was considerable in girth, and he had a big smile. His beard was big and full enough that he could play Santa Claus without a fake one (as he did). He had an unforgettably big, hearty voice.

But even with all these oversized attributes, his heart was still the biggest thing about him. It was this—his genuine love of people, his desire to see them as happy and fulfilled as he seemed to be—that led him into public service when he returned to Randolph after a 20-year career out-of-state.

It was this that led him to plunge into town affairs as selectman for four years, most of them as an energetic chairman. His spirit shone in the way he conducted those meetings, treating all who came before him with unfailing respect, whether he agreed with them or not, treating them also with the great good humor that rolled so easily out of him, and helped make him a natural leader and coalition-builder. That same impetus led him to serve at the state level, where his broad knowledge and quick mind landed him on the Appropriations Committee after just one term.

And it was pure heart that brought Jim together with Vermont Adaptive Ski and Sports program, which teaches handicapped people how to ski and provides special equipment for them. This would be the passion that drove him like no other for the last 10 years.

He roped his family into accompanying him on trips to Ascutney, then Pico and other ski areas almost every single week. He did it simply to help people widen their horizons of what they could accomplish while giving them a taste of the sport of skiing. And did he love to ski! Every year for years, Hutchinson put in 100 days or more on the ski slopes.

His love for the Adaptive Ski organization led him to become the organization's executive director for two years, though he refused to accept the paycheck that went with the job. He then put himself in charge of the VASS 100-Mile-Run, a fundraiser that was an enormous organizational effort that annually raised about $30,000 for VASS.

Jim Hutchinson's heart stopped beating this week Monday. It was much, much too soon, but before it shut down, that great heart had reached out to hundreds of individual people, had spread great dollops of enjoyment and good cheer, and had made Randolph, Vermont, and the world a better place.

VERMONT'S MASTER
OF THE AVANT GARDE

When the Bulgarian artist Christo ran a 15-foot high fence for miles across the Southern California landscape, he called it an art object.

When enormous bureaucratic squabbles broke out about Christo's right to put up a big fence in California, and particularly in the sacrosanct Californian ocean, Christo engagingly explained that the furor was part of the art object, too. Any way in which aesthetic concerns intersect with society at large is a kind of art project, he said.

Using this criteria, it appears that, unsuspected by anybody, the most significant avant garde artist on the Vermont scene may be Raymond Ramsey, a land developer who has brought aesthetic discourse to new heights of subtlety in Stowe.

Ramsey is the developer who was turned down on his Act 250 application to develop some farmland on the Mountain Road in Stowe and who responded by announcing that the conspicuous site would, instead, be a great place for a pig farm with up to 400 porkers.

This was Ramsey's first great aesthetic vision. Imagine a carload of out-of-staters driving the Mountain Road toward lofty Mt. Mansfield for the first time, passing miles of chic restaurants, hotels, lodges, real estate offices, theaters, ski rental establishments, and condominiums.

Imagine the visual impact on these tourists when they round a bend in the road, and there, peacefully grazing beside the banks of a crystal stream, are 400 fully-grown sows! Imagine the aesthetic excitement on the part of the youngsters in the car, the demands to stop the car and feed some McDonalds French fries to these glorious specimens of nature's most perfect eating machine!

Indeed, it must be said that Raymond Ramsey's vision makes Christo seem a pedant by comparison. For whereas Christo's lovely, billowing fence appealed solely to the eye, Ramsey's pigs are certain to afflict virtually all the senses of those who, as they say in California, experience the event. Not only will they see the pigs, they can hear 'em (the squalling of 400 pigs at feeding time must be a caution), they can touch 'em, they can contemplate tasting 'em, and they will most certainly be able to smell 'em. All in all, Raymond Ramsey's artistic vision for the Mountain Road represents a significant milestone in the annals of the American avant garde.

And Ramsey has been just as successful as Christo in bringing forth the other elements of the latter-day art project—an impact on the larger society and its institutions. The full array of Vermont's sophisticated land use bureaucracy has already been drawn into the fray, sparking all the hearings and petitions and employing all the lawyers one could hope for in a modern-day work of art.

Now, we are glad to report, Mr. Ramsey's initiative has provided artistic inspiration for others in the Stowe valley. As of this writing, a pig rodeo is being planned by a restauranteur, Harvey Schroll, on the Mountain Road. Ingeniously melding the avant garde techniques of Christo and Ramsey with the centuries-old tradition of the artist-as-entertainer, Schroll has scheduled a Piglet Beauty Contest, Greased Pig Contest, a Pig Race, and Hog Riding. Schroll has even managed to ignite a new furor, as the Central Vermont Humane Society has come down hard on the idea of a Pig Rodeo.

Whether Raymond Ramsey's great vision of 400 pigs rooting through the topsoil of the Ski Capital of the East will ever come to pass is now almost irrelevant. Merely by imagining his scenario he has engaged our imaginations, harnessed our energies. He is an artist indeed, and Vermont should be proud of him, even if he does come from Maine.

MATTHEW

At the intersection where
We used to have a traffic light,
Matthew had to halt his Massey Ferguson
At the brow of the Route 66 hill

And when his turn came
He tromped on the throttle
And that tractor came charging
Out of there into the crossing
Front wheels rearing up
Three feet above the pavement,
Matthew hallooing and also the kid
Hanging on alongside while
That 300 horsepower roared too.

I missed a gear back there,
He told me when I saw him later.

Maybe so.
But that wouldn't explain
The grin that wrapped nearly around his face
And the way his beard wagged to and fro
Before the front wheels
Hit the road again.

A PROMISE KEPT

Feature in the White River Valley Herald, July 13, 1978

Fifty-three years ago a young preacher, with his wife and son, moved to East Braintree (Snowsville) to begin his ministry. Two years later he moved away, and his parishioners promised never to forget him.

It was a promise that was kept. Through 51 years the people of the parish, which includes West Brookfield as well as East Braintree, never forgot Rev. C. Arthur Hazen and his wife Doris. During the years 1925 to 1927, bonds of love and affection grew so strong that they effortlessly spanned the five succeeding decades.

Last Sunday that 50-year span closed altogether for a few hours. Rev. and Mrs. C. Arthur Hazen returned to the church with the slanting steeple, and he preached again from the pulpit which had first echoed his words.

In the congregation were many whom he had addressed that first Sunday when, he confessed, he had told them everything he knew and had wondered what to preach about the following week.

Several were present from the Boy Scout troop he had formed. And some couples came whose hands he had clasped in wedding vows.

In all, the congregation numbered nearly 100, including old friends and new. The church was bright with flowers and greens, each arrangement affirming the constancy of the people of this rural parish.

The story of Sunday's service actually began more than a year ago when the Rev. Hazen, who lives in Swanton, was hospitalized for a hip operation. Several of his former Scouts heard the news and spread it to friends and former parishioners. Cards and letters poured in, together with $30 for flowers.

Touched, Rev. Hazen said he would like to thank his friends by preaching one more time in the two-church parish. The idea was grasped enthusiastically, and the organizing began.

A service was arranged by two members of the old Boy Scout troop, Keith Rogers and Willis Abel, and their wives, Mabel and Mae. A third former Scout, Francis Blanchard, helped Wilbert Bowen prepare a barbecue. Others attending from the troop included Everett Hoyt, Albert Fullam, and Grant Flint, who was married to his wife Lucy by Rev. Hazen in Norwich.

Amid the floral arrangements, some donated by parishioners and some by Edmunds Greenhouse, Rev. Hazen preached with the same resonance and directness which long ago had so affected the valley residents. Unaccompanied solos were sung by Mrs. Hazen and by Marjorie Drysdale, and congregational hymns, treasured favorites, rang through the sanctuary.

For the scripture, Rev. Hazen chose the Beatitudes. His sermon, entitled "Life Is an Adventure," was part reminiscence and part instruction in the life lessons, some of them hard, learned during a 50-year ministry in small Vermont towns.

Concluding, Rev. Hazen spoke warmly once again of the East Braintree and West Brookfield people and their faithfulness to the past; and he had one piece of advice:

"Bless the future," preached the Rev. Arthur Hazen. "The past must bless the future."

In Swanton, the blessing will be tangible. The donations intended to buy flowers during Rev. Hazen's convalescence arrived too late, and the $30 will be put to better use. The money will purchase flowers for a special garden near the minister's Swanton home, a garden which will be named for his loyal Scouts and parishioners in Central Vermont.

And so, flowers will bloom in a Swanton garden, as they did in the Snowsville church Sunday, fragrant with memories. Each year they will raise their heads again, a glad remembrance of the past, and a blessing for the future.

OVATION

Even as a novice landscaper, Zack
Understood at once why
He ought not carve neat arcs
Into the turf
Around my lawn maples.

In gratitude, the purple asters
Having stolen unbidden into
The barky spread of ancient roots,
Have just now burst
Into wild applause.

WES'S WISDOM

According to his obituary, Wes Herwig, who died last Wednesday [December 10, 2003], worked for 25 years for *The Herald*.

He sure did.

That flat statement, however, does little to indicate the role that Wes played at *The Herald*, during those 25 years and during the 25 or so years following. His influence here was enormous.

He started as a writer for the former publisher, John Drysdale, but his main job, which he was very good at, was as an advertising salesman. When Wes went out on his route every week, however, he did far more than collect ads. He had a sharp eye for news, and a great gift for getting people to talk, so every week he'd come back from his ad run with a story, or several stories, some of which he'd write up himself. Likely enough, he would come back with a good photo, too.

Just as important as collecting ads and news, Wes was spreading goodwill for *The Herald*. If the State Department had ambassadors like Wes Herwig to send out to foreign countries, the United States would be popular all over the world. Everywhere, Wes was welcomed and made himself useful.

Those wide contacts up and down the White River Valley made him especially valuable at *The Herald*. He felt the pulse of the Valley every week, and both the former publisher and the current one sought out his advice on any and all issues. Wes always spoke with the voice of common sense and deep understanding both of people and issues, and at *The Herald* we listened hard.

A few years after the current publisher took over in 1971, Wes began to ask to cut down his hours, and eventually left the job entirely. He had a lot he wanted to do—such as founding the Randolph Historical Society and establishing its museum; such as publishing books, 40 of them, under the Greenhills Press label. Such as creating his own books, one of which, "Early Photographs of Randolph," is in constant demand. Such as delving more and more deeply into Vermont history until he became acknowledged one of her finest local historians.

All of these retirement activities he carried on hand-in-hand with his wife Miriam, who shared all his passions and his cheerful spark for life. As historian Howard Coffin said in his eloquent eulogy Sunday, "it is impossible to speak of Wes Herwig without speaking of Mim Herwig. They were inseparable…"

Still, Wes and Mim continued to contribute mightily to the life of *The Herald*, and the White River Valley at large. All questions about Randolph in earlier times automatically went to the Herwigs. And at various and unexpected moments, a couple of times a year, would arrive on our doorstep a bright contribution to the newspaper about people and events in the past, usually written by Mim but reflecting Wes's interests and research as well. By a happy chance the most recent of those was published in *The Herald* on the day he died, a lively story, full of painstaking research and gentle humor, about the bells and bell-ringers at the Randolph Center church.

Finally, it was our good fortune that Wes continued to visit us. Days at *The Herald* can be hectic, and those who pass through our front door have every possible agenda.

No matter how busy we were, though, there never was a time that we weren't pleased as punch to see Wes Herwig walk through the door. The conversation might start in the past, but it would always range through the years to the present, always offering once again some thoughtful comment, or witty remark, or trenchant observation, all of which added up to the wisdom of Wes Herwig.

And whatever he said came packaged in such agreeable sincerity, such a zest for people and events, that you felt, even when he was in his eighties, that a fresh young breeze had just passed through the room.

THE DAY THE SUN CAME OUT

For ten days before this brief piece was written,
the Central Vermont skies had been unremittingly dark with
clouds. When it wasn't raining, it was threatening to rain.
As the editor walked across Randolph's Main Street bridge on
Wednesday, however, the clouds broke and a brilliant ray of
light pierced the soggy scene. As it happened, Wednesday
is publication day for The Herald, and the editor had still not
written an editorial, so he hurried back to the office and wrote one.

Just before noon Wednesday the strangest of sights appeared in the heavens over Central Vermont. People ran into the streets. Children screamed and held onto their mothers. Dogs howled and even the cattle in their stalls lowed anxiously. Citizens shielded their eyes as the strange glowing sphere in the sky spread a yellow light over the landscape. They shuddered as an unaccustomed warm sensation invaded their skin.

Only the old people were unshaken—they and a few history professors. "Oh yes," they said. "It is as of old. We used to call it The Sun." They turned their faces to the sky and let the light and warmth flood in. They smiled with nostalgic fulfillment.

Then the people rejoiced. They, too, spread their limbs and lifted their faces and basked in the sunlight. They looked with new eyes at a shining world, at mountain peaks, long hidden, now gleaming. At the end of the day, the brilliant sphere sank beneath the horizon. The old people said they remembered when the sun used to rise every day. But almost nobody believed them.

A Novice Aloft:
Riding the Phantom F-4D

White River Valley Herald, June 23, 1983

A voice crackled through the microphone in my helmet: "You'd better close your canopy now. It's the switch by your left elbow."

Sure, Okay. Switch by my left elbow. I looked down.

There were about 300 switches by my left elbow, a numbing maze of toggles, buttons, levers, and dials. Some had labels, but the letters were worn and obscure, and most were abbreviations. They might as well have been in Greek.

Among this sea of switches, where was the magic one which would close the plexiglass canopy over my head and keep me from blowing out of the airplane?

The headset crackled with more instructions. My pilot, Denis Leuders, was patient, but the other two planes were warming for takeoff. Wouldn't I please close my canopy? Already I was sweating inside my helmet and finding it hard to take a deep breath. Couldn't hear my instructions clearly. Connected to so many straps and tubes that I could scarcely move. I was getting the distinct impression that I had gotten myself into a situation that was more than I had bargained for.

It all started when I saw press photographs of the F-4D Phantom jet that the Vermont Air National Guard received in 1981, replacing EB-57s as its training planes. The F-4Ds are high performance fighter-bombers, manufactured by the thousands in the 1960s and 1970s, capable of flying 1800 miles an hour (Mach 2.2), and very maneuverable.

"Wouldn't it be fun to get a ride in one of those," I said to myself, as I scanned the photographs.

WRONG WORD

"Fun," as it turned out, was not the right word. "Exciting," yes.

The Vermont Air National Guard is technically the 158th Tactical Fighter Group of the Air Reserve, and its crews go by the name of "the Green Mountain Boys." This appelation decorates all of the planes, which were hangared in a special National Guard section of the Burlington Airport.

The commanders of the Guard apparently were glad to get the chance for a little publicity, and perhaps they were more than a little curious about what would happen when they strapped a novice into an F-4D. At any rate, I received a gracious invitation from Lt. Col. David L. Ladd, deputy commander of operations, who said the flight could be arranged.

I should plan on spending all day, Col. Ladd advised. There was a lot of training to go over. How to eject from an airplane, for instance.

That should have been a clue that a ride in an F-4D wouldn't be exactly like the placid hot air balloon ride I had taken four years ago. But I pressed on.

A lot of joking greeted my arrival at the airbase about 9 A.M. on a Thursday morning.

"Don't let him scare you," called one fellow during my ejection seat briefing. "The chance is only one in 100 of something happening."

Chances are that the last 99 runs had been flawless, too.

"Oh no," others feigned in mock horror when they found I had been assigned to fly with Leuders. They offered that he was into drugs, that he had to take heart attack pills.

Actually, it was soon clear that Denis was one of the stars in the small galaxy of pilots at the Air National Guard, the one to beat when it came to tallying hits on target. He even looked like a fighter pilot—tall, blonde, and fit, with piercing blue eyes which were not cool, exactly, but which seemed to see for a mile or so behind your head. The right stuff.

Three or four hours of pre-flight instruction passed surprisingly quickly. Much of it dealt with the layer upon layer of clothing parceled out to me by Paul Parent and Ed Blow. Besides my flight suit, I received an anti-G suit, a survival vest, and a harness with more survival equipment. "Survival," in fact, seemed to be a pretty important word.

The vest alone included a compass, a strobe light, a heat-resistant collar, 13 distress flares with a night end and a day end (red lava or orange smoke, respectively), a signal mirror, a police whistle, flashlight, tourniquet, jackknife, matches, a hunting knife, seven high flares, and more stuff that I was so busy learning how to use that I didn't have time to write down.

Standard issue also included two plastic bags, discretely inserted into paper bags. Should you need to use one, the instructions warned, to be sure to unbuckle your helmet first.

The harness (which straps you into the cockpit) contained more survival equipment nestled in the corners, including a needle and thread. And the ejection seat of the plane, I soon learned, had much more, including my life raft, a two-way radio, a can opener, sponges, and, of course, my parachutes.

FOUR PARACHUTES

Four parachutes, actually. Each of them pulls out the next one, while meantime your life raft inflates itself automatically and drifts lightly to the ocean or the treetops just before you.

I was almost beginning to think it might be fun to eject—until my briefing officer mentioned a few other facts: If my legs were not flat on the seat, he said, the force of the ejection might break them. If my back were not straight, then that might break, too. I was easily talked out of ejecting.

Even more fascinating was the Anti-G suit, which wraps tightly around your legs and lower torso and automatically inflates in five places when pressure in the cabin reaches two G's or more. One G is the force of gravity we all experience every day—and which our bodies are built for. When an airplane pulls out of a dive, it subjects the occupants to pressures several times the amount of gravity. That, in turn, tends to force the liquid blood into the feet and legs, just as water stays in the bottom of a pail when you swing it around your head.

Denis explained what happens when your blood is in your legs instead of in your head. "First you get tunnel vision," he said. "Then no vision at all, then you lose consciousness." Squeezing various anterior muscles helps the Anti-G suit to force the blood back into your head, he pointed out. So I practiced squeezing my muscles.

Of course, Paul Parent explained, there are many kinds of G's—negative G's (in a dive) and sideways G's (in a hard banking curve). I would feel a good variety of them, eventually.

Col. Ladd explained that I would be sent out on a routine training mission over Fort Drum in New York State. There, in the midst of acres of swamp, is a practice bombing range, with a half dozen targets for both bombs and strafing, and a system for recording how close the "bombs" (smoke charges, actually) come to the targets.

Before leaving, the three-man crews were briefed by the flight leader, Cap. Pete McInerney. He described the kinds of bombing runs which were to be practiced, and the crew filled in complicated formulas on their Mission Data cards. A code book as thick as Webster's dictionary told the pilots what bomb angle to use, depending on temperature, size and type of bomb, and other factors. As much guesswork eliminated as possible.

Most of what McInerny said consisted of code words and jargon that were incomprehensible to the uninitiated; the extent of the technical knowledge was impressive.

The flight leader also threw in a short quiz on safety procedures, and briefed the crew on various checkpoints for start-up. These were procedures the pilots had studied a dozen times, but the repetition was important; one couldn't be too familiar with safety rules.

He warned them against spatial disorientation while in their bombing maneuvers. "Believe the gauges more than you believe the seat of your pants," he cautioned.

"Keep both jets in sight at all times," the flight leader warned. "Keep out of 'coffin corner' situations."

We thought that sounded like a fine idea.

Seems Small

Moments later, we were in the hangar.

For someone like myself, used to the ponderous vastness of a Boeing 747, the Phantom F-4D seemed small. With a wing-span of only 58 feet and two engines tucked close to the fuselage, it is a tight, muscled piece of machinery. No flab.

Leuders walked me around the plane, pointing out the Sidewinder and smaller Sparrow air-to-air missiles. Under the nose nestled an instrument made famous in Vietnam days—a laser tracker to guide so-called "smart bombs" to their destination with uncanny accuracy.

Taxiing out to the runway was exhilarating, as the open canopy over my head let the wind run through my hair and the airport noises buzz through my brain.

"This is the way to fly," I told myself.

Then came the instructions to close the canopy and the fevered search for the right button. Leuders solved this one by leaning out of his seat and gesticulating until I found the troublesome button. Then we were on the runway.

Fire blazed from the belly of the plane as its G.E. Turbojet engines—each with a thrust of 17,000 pounds—sprang to life. In moments we, too, were hurtling down the runway, glued to the back of our seats, launched into the air in seconds and climbing steeply.

Wow! No sooner were we off the ground than we began a hard turn to the right, banked at a 30-degree angle, still climbing steeply. McInerny found a hole in the cloud cover, and we sprinted through it so that suddenly we were floating above the clouds, surrounded by brilliant blue. We closed to a loose formation, our two co-voyagers suspended beside us. Except for the passing of the clouds, we all might have been standing still in the air.

WING SIGNAL

McInerny dipped his wings, and the three planes closed quickly to the "fingertip formation," the wingtips of each plane seemingly only a few yards apart.

"This is probably about as close together as we get," I observed to Denis, consciously keeping any nervousness out of my voice.

"That's right," he agreed.

Suddenly, the formation broke abruptly. We veered left and down. For the first time, my Anti-G suit inflated. McInerny had given us a short exercise in evasive action.

"Want to handle the plane?" Denis asked. Or at least I think he did. Signals were coming over my headset from

Burlington, Boston, and McInerny as well as Denis, and I was having trouble sorting them out.

I touched the stick, and the Phantom veered abruptly to the left. Talk about power steering! The merest nudge forward, and we zoomed 100 feet above the rest of the formation.

Supersonic speed was out of the question—breaking the sound barrier is not allowed during these practice bombing runs and is limited to high altitudes. But still, I was assured, I would be able to see what the plane could do.

As we reached the boggy area of Fort Drum, we could see a little shack which was to be one of the targets, and we swung our pre-arranged routines.

Zip! The horizon disappeared as we turned in a tight circle. The ground was below us, the target somewhere underneath my right elbow. The Anti-G suit began to swell.

On line with the target the F-4D straightened again and headed down at a 20-degree angle until we seemed to skim the trees.

Wham! Denis pulled out of the attack angle quickly, and my body responded by trying to ooze through the floor of the airplane. My Anti-G suit inflated to full size. I felt as though I were buried in watermelons, with the biggest one sitting on my chest, congesting my breath.

In front of me, a clock-like dial told me that the pressure was up to four G's. I squeezed every muscle I had, hard.

The pressure didn't last long, though, and when it abated, I felt reassured. Not too bad. I can stand this.

The first exercise had been a 20-degree pass. The schedule for the day called for two of those, followed by two 10-degree runs, then two "10-degree pops," during which we would fly in close to the ground, rise quickly and dive again to deliver the payload, then veer away. Finally, a level bombing run—the most difficult for marksmanship—to be followed by a number of strafing passes for the Phantom's machine guns.

WHERE'S THE GROUND?

We banked steeply to get in position for the second 20-degree approach, resulting in some of the sideways G-forces they told me about. Interesting. Where was the ground, anyway? Oh, yes, there it was, in back of my head. I wondered why.

Denis was coming in again toward the target, the ground rushing to meet us. I tensed my muscles in anticipation this time, as the watermelons started to pile on.

No sooner had we pulled out than the Phantom tore around again in a sharp circle, ready for the 10-degree approach. I could see one of the other planes streaking along the ground, going much faster than we seemed to be. I was losing perspective, and I began to realize that I wasn't having any "fun."

The Phantom straightened for another approach, but only briefly. Down we went again, then up, then around. The motion was constant and so was the G-pressure, in one form or another. The horizon was always in a funny place. I realigned my goals from having fun to getting back home with my breakfast still in place.

When your stomach starts to act up, pure oxygen helps, the ground crew had told me. I had turned my air to pure oxygen sometime after the first bombing approach.

I think it was the 10-degree "pops" that did me in— the relentless banking turn, then down, up, down, and then hard up again to escape the imaginary flak.

I had already begun to experiment with my helmet, making sure I could get the mask off if the need arose. Mercifully, I got it off in time, although I had been jovially warned that I would not be the first to despoil my helmet and oxygen mask, should I be so unfortunate.

Somewhere in that first "pop" I lost my breakfast, then yesterday's dinner, then lunch. I tried to do it loudly so that Denis, hearing my predicament, might fly the airplane straight for a mile or so.

Finally, I was able to put my helmet back on. "You should feel better now," he said, not unkindly. I did, too.

But meanwhile, he continued to turn the plane in circles and up and down in dizzying ways. I could not believe that he was able to do these crazy things with the Phantom and still coolly release his bombs at the right instant, at the right angle. Here I was, trying just to survive the next dive, while he was surveying the horizon, steering the plane, dropping the bombs, and probably even watching the radar. My admiration for him and all the others rose about 30 notches.

900 POUNDS

At the end of one of the runs, Denis gave the stick an extra nudge backwards. The meter read five G's. For a few seconds, I weighed 900 pounds!

Suddenly, finally, the horizon subsided into a straight line below us. My Anti-G suit deflated, and we were on our way home. It was a lovely trip, but somehow I did not enjoy it as much as the ride out. As we approached the Queen City of Burlington, my stomach remembered something it had forgotten.

Tall thunderheads stood piled over the lake, but we wove our way between them to the ground.

The ground felt good. Taking off my helmet felt good. Taking off the Anti-G suit felt REALLY good.

The pilots were gathered in the debriefing room, and it was easy now to understand the aura around them, the sense of being a select society. They rehashed the exercise, received word on whose bombs had scored and whose had not.

There had been one bullseye, while most of the rest of the "bombs" had fallen 8 to 30 yards from the targets. On the level runs, however, the closest bomb had been 51 yards from the target, underscoring the difficulty of this approach. For each exercise, the most on-target crew won a quarter, while the crew whose "bombs" had fallen farthest from the mark lost an equal amount.

Denis's strafing had been marvelous, in spite of the fact that he had cut it short one run because of an incapacitated passenger. For his efforts, we won two quarters, and according to custom, we split the take. I put mine towards a deposit on a fix of Alka-Seltzer.

Denis pocketed his quarter and sauntered back onto the tarmac for another flight.

VT/VT

*On April 16, 2007, a lone gunman terrorized the campus of
Virginia Tech. The toll was 32 dead and 17 wounded.*

It came as a shock, as we tuned into the television
coverage of Sunday's shooting, to see the placards around
the bereaved campus emblazoned with the letters "VT."

Of course, of course—the college where the tragedy
occurred was Virginia Tech, and of course its nickname
was VT. Still, when we turned on the television and saw
all those VT signs, we thought for a moment that we
were watching a program about ourselves, about our
Vermont, our VT.

And—of course—it turned out that we were. We were
indeed watching a show about us, about ourselves. Not
a show about something that happened somewhere else,
to someone else, but a terrible drama about things that
had happened—were happening—to us. To our children.
To our America. To our humanity.

It was impossible to separate the events that transpired
Sunday morning at VT from our own world in VT. The
scene was so familiar: this place of learning, these young
people so full of fun and seriousness and life and promise.
We knew them before we were even told who they were.
They were our children.

We knew these parents. Some of them, as they sent
their young folks off to college, remembered fondly
their own campus days, the laughter and the stimulation,
the new worlds to discover. They hoped for the same for

these young souls, waited eagerly for their return each vacation to hear of more adventures, which stirred memories of their own. And some of these parents, who had not had the privilege themselves, had felt perhaps a little anxious as they left their young at these gates of promise, entering a world a bit strange to them, to prepare themselves for the larger world, which was called the future.

We even knew the murderer. He was the young man with the blank stare, who seemed namelessly different from other people, who spoke seldom and poorly, but nursed something inside, something hard, something huge, that alarming youth whose eyes were impenetrable from without, unseeing from within.

We all had encountered this young man, within whom something did not click, who had connected only with the disconnected but continuous stream of inhumanity that pours from the ether of our culture, some of it actual news of the world, some of it manufactured for our taste, as if we craved more conflict and alienation, as if there were not trouble enough already abroad in the land.

Unspeakable events like the one at Virginia Tech have exploded often enough now that we know them indeed. In fact, we own them. We own the unbearable individual sadnesses, the general despair, the incomprehensibility of it all. We own also a nagging revulsion for what this nation of promise has harbored, hoping that this is not what we have become.

Yes indeed. VT is VT.

OCTOBER 21, 2003

Fair portal to the dimmest
Third of the year
And also the appointed day

When autumn steps entirely
Out of her brilliant cloak,
Draping it at our feet

So that we can scarcely draw a breath
For sheer amazement
At yesterday's unruly lawn
Today resplendent: all
The summer's fallen wealth
Blazing upward in
Retrospective salute.

Warm breezes have recruited sweet
Traces of wood smoke to chase the last
Leafy shreds tumbling in showers
From their twigs. What else
Could be needed this day—unless

A cat on my shoulder? The black one
Obliges, settles close to my ear.
Stiffens with the next gust, batting out
As a leaf spirals close,
Tail lashing my cheek.

Above, high clouds race eastward
Pell mell, dragging behind them
The hard face
Of November.

Driscoll Reid

*This October 7, 1999 letter was in response to
the funeral of Driscoll Reid, as sent to his wife, Ellen Reid.
Driscoll was the family dentist, a neighbor,
and served for years on the Randolph School Board,
along with my mother Eleanor Drysdale.*

Dear Ellen,

I'm not much for crying at funerals, but I had a hard time with that one. I didn't hear many of the nice words or sing the music very well. I found I carried an empty space inside. Something important was gone that had been there, something solid, something to depend on.

What a rock Driscoll was for us of the younger generation! What a paragon of good sense and competence! What a font of interesting thoughts and ideas! What a dependable source of charity and understanding!

Especially was he so for me, not only from my personal connection but from my mother's regard for Driscoll. How well I remember the school board talk, the determination to work for progressive ends while respecting the people who saw things differently. They were great allies, my mom and your husband, and they left a great legacy to this town.

It's his voice that I may remember longest. His voice at the dental chair or in the next office, his voice in conversation, or reasoned argument. It was such a reassuring voice, so deep that it always felt grounded in reflection. It was a voice that sparkled with humor or was firm in conviction. A voice of wonderful kindliness, whether you received it as a child in his chair or as an adult.

I miss Driscoll more than I ever imagined I would, and so I can barely fathom what his loss means to you, Ellen. But what memories he has left behind, and how lucky we all were to know him!

Love,
Dick Drysdale

HAROLD

*Harold Luce of Chelsea was a legendary fiddler who played
100 gigs a year well into his nineties. He taught generations of
fiddlers from his modest home on Chelsea's Main Street,
and his stories were a welcome part of every lesson.*

*Harold has some advice
for players who please themselves
with the speed of their
bow hands.*

*The fiddle should serve
The feet, he says. He plays
Two hundred dances a year.*

*You got to have six speeds, Harold says,
And you'll be all set
as a fiddle player.*

*If they're promenading on
a hard floor
     is one.
Put down a rug, though, they
don't step so quick
     that's two
Move outside on the driveway
     that's three*

And if there's gravel there,
That slows 'em down some
    that's four.
A big lawn party on the grass—well
    that's five

And I didn't think I would
Need no more speeds than five
But you know
That one time after
a wedding they held   ·
their dance in a potato patch.

You can imagine. A potato patch, y' know
And I played for that, too
    And that's six.

Violin Virtuosity at Chandler

*New York City violinist Arturo Delmoni
performed at Chandler Music Hall on October 9, 2006.*

Dear Arturo,

I want to thank you personally for one of the most
wonderful evenings that I have ever spent in Chandler
Music Hall. I have spent a lot of them, having been
privileged to attend most of the musical offerings there
for the last 30 years, but Saturday night will remain
close to my heart.

I really don't know where to start. The Vivaldi was
the perfect opener, those sweeping arpeggios brimming
with the sheer joy of being a violin player in Italy in the
1700s. The Beethoven was perfect.

The Brahms was more than perfect; it's long been
one of my favorite pieces but only from disk; I didn't
imagine I would ever hear it played, to say nothing of
hearing it played so well. The slow movement of that
sonata must be the high point of any concert at which it
is ever played, and certainly it was Saturday night. I was
on the edge of my seat every second. The Debussy was
new territory for me, such a long journey for the instrument from its beginnings with Vivaldi and Corelli, but
such a rewarding exploration of sound and form.

And then you and your violin spent the rest of the
evening having fun!

I have to say I adore everything about your playing—
the conceptual framework, the interpretations, the

phrasings, the forthrightness, the care you take with every note, and above all that gorgeous tone, or rather such a rich cluster of tones, as there are so many facets to your tone. And to hear this—the full, full sound of the lower strings and the brilliant pearls of the highest notes so perfectly enunciated—to hear this in that beautiful hall in my own home town was almost more than I could bear, so that when you began "Deep River" the dam broke. As you had planned, I suspect.

It is always risky to suggest a comparison to another artist, but I will say there is something in your playing that reminded me of the Chandler performance, very late in her career, by the cellist Elsa Hilger. It was something in the simplicity of the approach: nothing comes between the listener and the music. No ego, no quirks, no undue dramatization, no odd body movements, and of course no technical issues at all. And the tone that seems impossible to issue from spruce and horsehair— Elsa had that, too.

As you know, we have had some decent fiddle players in Chandler recently—Jaime Laredo in the Beethoven concerto a couple of weeks ago, Adela many times, and Midori a few years ago. But it is you whose playing has brought me the most joy, and I thank you. I am glad the rest of the audience seemed as affected as I was; perhaps we can have you back.

Sincerely,

Dick Drysdale

INNOCENCE AND GUILT

*The fatal stabbings of Dartmouth professors
Half and Suzanne Zantop at their New Hampshire home in
2001 was widely met with disbelief and revulsion, and nowhere
more so than in Orange County, as two high school students
from Chelsea were charged with the crime. This editorial was
written early in the case, before the details were known.*

It is safe to say that never has the principle "innocent
until proven guilty" been more fervently invoked than
it has been this week by the people of Chelsea.

An almost palpable sense of dread settled over all of
Central Vermont as people tried to make sense of the
terrible charges levied by New Hampshire authorities
against two high school teenagers, two kids who seemed,
from all reports, not much different from any other high
school boy in Vermont.

Robert Tulloch and James Parker were bright lads,
thoroughly engaged in school and community activities.
They had healthy outside interests such as rock climbing,
and seemed to meet life with good humor. Parker was
invariably described as the "class clown," while Tulloch,
who had been elected student council president as a
junior, was described by one teacher as "charm itself."

The murder they are charged with is as gruesome as
any in the history of northern New England. The families
of the victims, joined by the entire Dartmouth community, are swimming in grief.

Now a wrenching trial of waiting has been imposed.
If the charges are proven to be true, a great deal more

pain will have to be endured, and not only by the people closest to the event. All Vermont is watching. Indeed, as Chelsea people know well by now, the entire nation is watching.

And for good reason. In the guilt or innocence of these two boys it is impossible not to read a tale of larger proportion. We are all hoping against hope. It's as if Innocence itself is at stake on the picturesque twin greens of Chelsea, and nothing is as precious to us as that.

Randolph's Family Doctor

For a couple of generations of Randolph residents, Dr. Jim Woodruff stands in the center of memory. His passing last week doesn't change that.

He was an accomplished surgeon whose technique and example set high standards for the Gifford Hospital surgery suite. State health planners ran into that tradition of excellence when they tried to shut down the surgical department several years ago, claiming that a hospital as small as Gifford might be offering sub-par surgery. The storm that erupted over that bureaucratic effort was immediate and subsided only when the state hastily backed down.

Such was his reputation for technical excellence that he helped attract other fine physicians to Gifford. His example showed them that top-notch skills would not be wasted in a small community, that the people of Central Vermont deserved the best of medical care. Gifford's continuing preëminence as a small medical center with excellent doctors is indebted to the standards set by Dr. Woodruff.

He was, as Dr. Ronald Gadway said at Sunday's funeral, the last of the old-time docs in the Randolph area. Along with his contemporaries, Dr. Bill Angell and Ransom Tucker, he was the epitome of a family doctor. He held office hours, made house calls, delivered babies, practiced internal medicine—all the while serving as chief surgeon.

Even as poor eyesight pushed him to an early retirement, Dr. Woodruff continued to contribute, establishing a cancer registry here and contributing hours of his time to screening clinics and blood drives.

Still, it isn't his qualifications or his busy schedule that linger in memory. As Rev. Kathy Eddy said in her eulogy Sunday, it is Dr. Jim's smile that we remember him by. We remember it from the earliest times when we visited his Maple Street home office for a series of childhood shots, the smile that made a welcoming place out of a physician's office, the smile that assured a child that he was in good hands despite a little temporary pain.

We saw much more of that smile through adolescence and early adulthood, a smile that looked right past illnesses and injuries, right into the heart. There was never a doubt but that it was the whole patient being treated, not his or her particular complaints of the day.

We remember also the sadness in those same eyes when the time came for Dr. Jim to tell us that our mother, the former associate publisher of *The Herald* and a close friend, was terminally ill of cancer at an untimely age. We were not alone in our grief, the eyes said, and it helped.

What is striking, upon reflection, is that the sadness in Dr. Woodruff's eyes was of a piece with the famous smile. Both expressions took him deeply inside his patients, sharing and understanding. The depth of his appreciation for life was related to his grief at its passing, but there was no sense of anger or betrayal. Life and death are cut from the same cloth, and Dr. Jim admired the whole fabric.

Certainly, he wove wonderful raiment out of the pieces of fabric allotted to him, and wore it with grace and humility.

Remote

Yesterday, I saw a mom
Who used a remote control
On her kid.

She had him out for a walk, and
Being about five,
He explored ahead of her,
Off to one side and then the other
While she trudged down the middle
Of the path, eyes fixed
On the black plastic oblong
In her hand.

Never would he stray
Into the road, and when he ventured
A ways onto somebody's lawn,
He always turned right back.
She used the right and left
Arrows, I suppose.

On closer inspection you could see
She had a whole battery of buttons including
One that was inscribed
I DON'T THINK SO;
And you could just make out
The tear in the little boy's eye.

ANNUAL MEETING OF ECCENTRICS

*The following was written November 14, 2004 as a personal letter
to a longtime friend, a Randolph native and accomplished poet,
John Spaulding. Its subject is the 2004 annual meeting of
the New England Writers in Windsor, to celebrate
the publication of its annual anthology of poetry.*

Dear John,

Perhaps the snowstorm Saturday was a blessing; on
the other hand, if you are looking for colorful material
you would have found it at 151 Main Street.

The Anthology of New England Writers is, as far as I
can see, a respectable collection, drawn from writers all
over the country, most of whom have published in other
journals here and there. I liked some of the entries quite
a lot; I'll send you a copy.

The sponsoring organization, New England Writers,
however, is a caution, as they used to say. It is the personal creation of one Frank Anthony, who came to
Windsor in the 70s and was one of the founders of the
excellent Vermont Public Radio. 151 Main Street is an
exquisite, very old house that clearly hasn't had anything
done to it since Frank moved in but which is infested
with books and interesting artwork everywhere. We
(Marjie and I) were met at the door by Susan, who informed us she is Frank's third wife. Susan has the air of
someone who spends a great deal of her time making
eccentrics feel at home. She was lovely.

Sure enough, inside in the main room, about twenty-two eccentrics were seated in straight back chairs around the very edge of the room, with some cashews in the middle. I am inclusive in this description, because it seemed that merely being in the room made one an eccentric, regardless of whether one was when one walked in. A couple of the folks appeared to have crossed over the line and were quite mad.

As we all introduced ourselves, one man muttered only that he read books and walked around his house and read books, and the woman next to him gave a three-minute soliloquy about her inadequacy in every-thing. Oddly, several people in he room said they didn't belong there; even more oddly, I felt that I did.

Partway though the introductions an older man with a white ponytail came in with a well-dressed attractive woman. Asked if she was his wife, he boomed out: "No, she's only in training. Hasn't made the grade yet."

Even though you'll notice that the thirty-six poets published in the anthology come from all over, with only eight from Vermont, this crowd was mostly Ver-monters or from over the river in New Hampshire, and most of them knew each other. There were a few new people, including me and a normal-looking young man from Burlington who had won second place, and who was clearly proud but curious and then bemused as to what sort of society he had acquired such a prominent place in. The actual academics who judge the contest were not within leagues of the place.

94

We had all been invited to the "unveiling" of the Anthology, and that is just what happened next. It was the 17th Anthology that the New England Writers have published, and as proof of such, Frank produced a forest of some 17 candles, each a little shorter than the last. He also produced the 17 anthologies. The folks sitting next to me were deputized as candle lighters, and as Frank brought out each anthology from the past, he talked a little about it (mostly about the cover), and the deputies lighted another candle. Eventually, there was a considerable little bonfire burning there on the table. When we came to the pristine, virgin 17th candle, Susan swooped in with a box full of copies of the latest anthology, draped with not one but two gauze cloths, for the Unveiling. Frank said the appropriate words, the deputies attempted to light a candle and unveil the box at the same time, and we all clapped. I felt that having been deprived of being a Mason or a Granger—and not being a Catholic— I finally had a chance to be present at a presentation of a bona fide Marvel.

Those of us who were both in the anthology and present then read our poems. Frank told us we should be sure to put this day's reading in our resumes. Then we were asked to read anything else we had to share, and a few people did, including both the mad poets. Then Frank began to present his theories of many things, most notably his health, until Susan gently refused to divulge his latest blood pressure readings.

Then the poet with the wife-in-training demanded to solve the problem of what is poetry, and what is prose. At that, Marjie and I decided to leave. Susan seemed alarmed and said we *couldn't*, but it turned out she just wanted an official photograph. Most everybody heaved a sigh of relief that the poetry/prose conversation was over and it was time for some very excellent home-made refreshments courtesy of Susan.

So that's what you missed on Saturday. And on Sunday you missed a very excellent work party involving me and three Germans moving four cord of wood from my maple forest to my back yard.

—Dick

DICK MALLARY

Richard Walker Mallary, who represented Vermont in the
United States House of Representatives from 1972 to 1975,
farmed the rich Orange County soils of Fairlee before embarking
on impressive careers in both government and business.
He resided in Brookfield at the time of his death
in 2011 at the age of 82.

If you wanted to know much about Dick Mallary,
he'd be the last person to ask.

You'd never know, if you were around him casually,
that he was a summa cum laude graduate of Dartmouth.

If you asked him a question about agriculture, you'd
get an eager, knowledgeable response, but you wouldn't
know that for 20 years he ran perhaps the finest dairy
farm in Orange County, on lush Connecticut River
Valley fields in Fairlee.

If you asked him about state or local politics, you'd
get solid, reasoned opinions (he never lacked for opinions), but you wouldn't necessarily discover that Dick
had held about every important government job, elected
or appointed, in Vermont with the exception of the gov-
ernorship. You'd not be told, for instance, that he started
as town selectman, served both in the Vermont Senate
and the House—including two terms as speaker of the
house. Or that as administration secretary he was the
glue that held two separate administrations together.

Surely you wouldn't find out, unless you asked, that
he served a term in Washington as Vermont's only
Congressman during the 1970s.

And so far, we've covered only two of Mallary's full-time careers—as dairyman and public servant. After coming home from Washington, he made a seamless transition to the business sector, and once again cream rose to the top, as he became a top executive with both CVPS and VELCO.

No, you wouldn't have found out about any of these things from direct conversation with Dick Mallary. What you would have found instead was a soft-spoken acuity about public matters, a gentle sense of humor, a love of climbing mountains, and a steady, thoughtful moderation that made clear just why he was elected so many times by so many people.

He will be greatly missed.

ADAM'S BIRTHRIGHT

Adam is six months old
And has been brought
To Church. He is alone
With his father in a bright
Corner and cannot abide his ignorance
Of the light there, fractured
By the stained glass.

One thing I have asked of the Lord—
That will I seek after

Tiny arms and
Infant muscles notwithstanding,
Adam forces himself away,
Apart, from his father's chest
Flings his head
Toward the kaleidoscopic puzzle,
Hungry for it. Voracious.

That I may dwell in the house of the Lord
All the days of my life

In the chancel, the service has begun
And we are instructed that we
Belong to God.

But Adam
Is having none of it. He would
Own the light, own the color
Own the strong arm that
Holds him close,
Own the sweet air.

To behold the beauty of the Lord

Adam's eyes are big as saucers
Insatiable as the satellite dish
On the back lawn.

And inquire in his temple.

Adam chews a corner of the
Service calendar. Another gift
From God.
He relaxes a bit into
The huge chest, stiffens suddenly,
Lunges again toward the window—perhaps
He has just discovered
Blue.

Behold the beauty of the Lord
And inquire in his temple.

Dedicated to Adam Leicher, b. July 18, 2003
in Randolph, VT. Excerpts from Psalm 27.

So You Took Your Kid on Vacation...

We couldn't say that we hadn't been warned.

As summer approached, more than one of our acquaintances had smilingly told us not to expect much rest on our vacation—not with an 18-month-old boy in tow.

We had heard of parents who struggled home from an attempted vacation, exhausted and frustrated. Tales of interrupted schedules, new beds, changes in routine that could be accommodated neither by the infants nor by the parents, a fragile normalcy shattered by a week's search for Rest and Relaxation.

But we remained confident. The stories didn't sound like our child. No sir, Not Our Boy.

These musings wandered through my anguished head sometime between 1 and 2 A.M. as I drove round and round and round Mirror Lake in Lake Placid, N.Y. early last week. It was vacation, and Our Boy was seated behind me in the car seat, as awake as awake could be.

It turned out that a new bed and room in a mountain hiking lodge had indeed scuttled the inclination of Our Boy to sleep his usual 10 hours. The new location, plus the excitement of a moosehead in the living room and the attention of scores of novel faces, all meant that the younger generation was not only awake, but was bent on communicating his awakeness to everyone in the lodge. Thus, the late-night car trip. It lasted two hours before his eyes finally glazed and closed, only minutes before his father's did the same.

And then, there were the mealtimes. The lodge did not, of course, schedule meals at the whim of a toddler, making it necessary that Our Boy eat first and watch us eat later.

As it happens, 18-month-olds do not like to watch other people eat. They insist on playing with the utensils, the cups, the plates, and, of course, the food itself. They care little whether the desired object or substance is possessed by the parents or perhaps by a New Yorker who wants to Rest and Relax and may just not appreciate Our Boy.

"Don't worry about it; we'll clean it up," said a young woman of the crew. She was smiling, but we parents, crawling inside with embarrassment, knew for a certainty that the moment our backs were turned, the smile would turn to disgust.

His First Tantrum. Admirable. Shows crucial progress toward becoming two. Ah—an emerging sense of self.

His Second Tantrum. OMG, what do we do with him now?

We took Our Boy to several restaurants, so as to spread around the privilege of his presence during meals. At the steak place he saw his first ear of corn, thought it was a banana, which he detests, and threw it on the floor. Mostly, he ate and played with the ice cubes until they melted and mixed horribly with the rest

of the food on his tray. We left the congealed mess on
the high chair, along with a big tip, and slunk away.

The lodge itself was most amusing, though perhaps
not amused. Imagine the delight upon finding out that
the stalls in the Ladies' Room had doors which you
could crawl under! Imagine the consternation of the
occupant thereof when Our Boy suddenly appeared in
her compartment!

Before the arrival of Our Boy, the lodge possessed
three 1000-piece jig-saw puzzles. It now owns one
3000-piece puzzle.

With all of that, how can we ever explain that our
vacation was a big success? How to evoke the wonder in
his eyes and voice when he first saw that moosehead,
the astonished little voice piping, "Big Deer!"

Or how describe the first day's walk, when we
rounded the bend to discover a 50-foot ledge standing
before us—the little jump of surprise in the backpack,
the amazed voice again in our ear: "Big stone!"

The scenes in the high chair are easily eclipsed by the
mind's vision of the little one dressed for a rainy day
hike, arms and head poking through a white garbage
bag, eating fresh blueberries and exclaiming "Wet tree!"
as we clumsily brushed through the rain-laden
branches. Equally indelible is the recollection of a foggy
promontory: Our Boy sitting on the rock, still in his
backpack, a leaf clutched in one hand and a fern in the
other, treasured mementos of the hike up.

Our friends were right: Don't take your 18-month-old on your vacation if you expect Rest and Relaxation. You won't get much of it.

But who wants to rest when there is so much to learn? Who can relax when the natural universe is opening itself, leaf, bud and stone, to the eyes of an enchanted child?

Johnny Cunningham's
Chandler Finale

From The Herald of Randolph, December 25, 2003

One of the last concerts played by the great Scottish fiddle player Johnny Cunningham, who died last week of a heart attack at the age of 46, took place in Chandler Music Hall.

Cunningham played one of the final sets at the 2003 New World Festival on August 31st. It was the third time he had played at the Music Hall and his turn on the Chandler stage was momentous, a tour de force.

First he congratulated the Randolph area for appreciating fiddlers so much. "Fiddle capital of the world," I think he said—a considerable exaggeration but a warm acknowledgement of the appreciation for traditional music here.

He said he would begin his set by playing an old song he had learned as a child. He didn't know just what he would play after that: "I think I'll play some music I usually wouldn't," he said, "because I think this audience will appreciate it." We took that as a great compliment.

Then Johnny tucked in his fiddle, and he played for fifty straight minutes—without a break. No sooner would one lovely song die away than another would slyly take its place, maybe a jig or old-fashioned strathspey. Then came tender quiet songs, including my grandmother's favorite, the Skye Boat Song: "Speed, bonny boat, like a bird on the wing…"

It was as if he could not stop the flow of music within him, and the audience was rapt and dead silent. It was an historic moment in the old Music Hall. It was the night that Johnny Cunningham couldn't stop playing.

Now that he is gone, we feel again the magnitude of his bequest, and we are grateful.

Automotive Orchestra
Debuts in Rochester

*Laurie Anderson eventually became nationally known as one of
the first to popularize the phrase "performance art,"
but when this was written in 1972, she was unknown.*

The Village Green of Rochester is the loveliest setting
one could imagine for the world's first concert of works
written exclusively for massed automobile horns.

The tranquil green, bordered by neat white homes
and surrounded by steeply-rising hills, was the scene for
the unique concert last Sunday afternoon, August 27,
because Rochester is the only (or at least the first)
community in the nation to host its own Horn and
Engine Society.

Formed by young part-time residents of the town
(population 1100), the Rochester Horn and Engine
Society assembled ten autos of several makes and vary-
ing vintage before a curious audience of perhaps 50
people and presented "An Afternoon of Automotive
Transmission."

No less curious than the audience was the music.
Written especially for the tonal capabilities of the exact
autos represented, it was limited to seven notes; and
because the Fords all tooted in thirds, the harmonic
construction was limited.

Some of the instruments offered compensating
features, however. A Saab, for instance, used triple-
tonguing, and the quality of the musical sounds varied

from the Mickey Mouse beep of a motorcycle to the smooth, well-tuned blares of the modern American cars.

The three composers represented in the concert were ingenious at finding rhythmic and melodic devices to exploit their musical medium. Laurie Anderson, in particular, by her two offerings, has been catapulted to recognition as the world's foremost composer of works for automotive orchestra.

In a a particularly stunning touch, her "Concerto for Landrover with Six-Cylinder Back-Up" ended with a full chorus of all the auto horns, regardless of pitch, rising to a dramatic crescendo—an effect with which city residents may be familiar but which in the verdant Vermont setting achieved startling drama.

Ms. Anderson, who was primarily responsible for Sunday's concert, explained that the idea of an automotive orchestra occurred to her after she attended a fireworks display. To show appreciation (or impatience), the practice was for the audience to toot their auto horns, and Ms. Anderson was impressed by the variety of the tones and the pleasing character of some of them.

Sensing the germ of a major Happening, she posted a notice asking car owners to stop by for an audition. When the response was negligible, she took to the streets with a tape recorder, asking startled local motorists to toot into her machine. After gathering about 50 sample toots, Ms. Anderson eliminated the incongruous and overlapping sounds and assembled her instruments.

There was only one rehearsal. The scores composed by Ms. Anderson and two friends were color-coded in seven colors representing each available note. During the performance, the cars were lined up on the green (through permission from the town fathers), facing an antique bandstand where many of the spectators gathered under threatening skies.

Protruding through the sunroof of an ancient vehicle, each composer directed his or her own work, pointing in rhythmic motion at a master color chart. The musicians were amateur, but the rules were simple: "Just know your color and stick to it," instructed Ms. Anderson.

Peter Schneider, attired in a full tuxedo with black tie but without socks, directed his "Horn Pipe for Horn and Pipe" while Geraldine Pontius conducted her "Well-tempered Beep." Besides her Landrover concerto, Ms. Anderson offered "L'auto-da-fe: Six-Part Fugue for the Well-Fueled Heretic."

The Landrover concerto was flawed by the non-appearance of the Landrover, which was out of state, but few could tell the difference. The absence of another vehicle sent the organizers scurrying down the line of assembled spectators, blowing their auto horns until an E-natural was found and pressed into service.

In an expression of purpose on the mimeographed program, the Rochester Horn and Engine Society explained that "the performers and composers hope to demonstrate that car horns have dimensions other than those of noise pollutants and nerve irritants."

"The car with its loud noises and pungent smells has invaded every small town in America: we do not aim to bring urban sounds to the country, but simply to bring some temporary order to this ever-increasing stream of sounds."

120 Years of Printing

*Editorial written after The Herald bowed to
financial realities and began sending each weekly issue
to The Valley News of West Lebanon to be printed.*

Readers will have already noticed that this week's edition of *The Herald* differs significantly from its predecessors. The four-color photograph on page one is something readers have never seen before in *The Herald*. The width of the paper, too, has changed to thirteen and three quarters inches, now a standard in the newspaper industry.

Both changes come about as a result of the larger change announced last week. For the first time in 120 years, this week's *Herald* was not printed at its own plant in Randolph.

There's a sadness about that on many levels. Brought up as a *Herald* brat, our earliest memories of the place have to do with the smells and the sounds of the production process, not the niceties of editing. A ten-year-old boy isn't stirred by such aspects of journalism as news judgment and lead writing. Such a boy is, however, entranced by the spit of an errant drop of lead as it hits the floor, the incredible variety show of a Linotype in action, the maneuvering of 1000-pound rolls of paper, the heavy exhilarating efficiency of a press printing 250 copies a minute of a 16-page newspaper, each neatly folded.

Even in our relatively adult twenty-plus years as publisher, a good many of the memories relate to the physical process of printing the paper. There was the cranky folding machine which looked as if it were designed by Rube Goldberg and required an operator with almost mystical intuition about what the machine was going to do next. There were a couple of late night breakdowns when it became an even question whether *The Herald* was going to publish or not, each time solved by the pressman in the nick of time.

Except for the Vermont Castings Dis-a-matic at the foundry, our newspaper press may have been the biggest single machine operating in Randolph. Big machines gather a mystique and personality about them—and they also tend to attract a particular kind of person as operator. People who run newspaper presses not only have to be mechanical geniuses, they also need a reservoir of patience, great attention to detail, and a willingness to deal with any new problems that the press has just thought up for them. With all of those requirements, a sense of humor seems a necessity for the job, too.

The Herald, and this publisher, have been fortunate to have pressmen—"Pete" Cooper, Guy Waldo, Dick Huggard, and Bruce Dickinson—with all those qualities in abundance.

So there's a sense of loss at *The Herald* this week, a loss of tradition and old-style independence and all the wonderful ways that the printing process assaulted the senses. Most important, a human loss.

The printing business is changing as quickly as any in our economy. Long ago, the hot lead of the Linotypes and Ludlow casting machines of our earliest memories were rejected in favor of the lighter, cheaper, higher quality processes of offset printing. This newspaper was the first in Vermont to make the revolutionary switch to offset printing in 1960 under former publisher John Drysdale.

And the unmistakable trend now, directed by economics, is for printing to take place at central printing facilities. Weekly newspapers, in particular, seldom print their own papers anymore; in Vermont, only one weekly still is self-printed—the *News & Citizen* in Morrisville. *The Herald* has kept its own printing facility much longer than most, but this week we join the majority.

For our readers and advertisers, this switch will not mean a loss of service or excellence. As the splash of color on page one shows, change brings new opportunities. But we won't deny the nostalgia. The acrid odor of hot metal is long absent from our 95-year-old offices on Pleasant Street. We've missed it for 30 years. We'll miss the smell of the ink and the busy roar of the presses even more.

Art Upstages Office
at Marlboro Festival

*Published in the Springfield Union
of Springfield, Massachusetts, Summer 1967*

It was the last place you would think of looking for a
vice-president. Marlboro, Vermont, has a population
which has been generously estimated at 300, and as one
drives through its center, there is not even a general
store—only a white church, fire station, a tiny art museum
and a Post Office in a home.

The town is surrounded by dairy pastures of the
most idyllic stamp on the sides of hills that make such
farming less than lucrative. Another asset is small, independent Marlboro College—and another is Marlboro
Music Festival.

It was the festival Sunday that attracted Vice President
Hubert H. Humphrey, along with generous numbers of
security men and members of the press.

The concert hall itself is only a rude shelter pitched
in a pasture, and the dozens of brown-suited state
troopers who were on hand as early as two hours before
the concert seemed utterly incongruous in the pastoral
landscape.

Assisting the state troopers and the secret service-
men in imposing "security" were several local officials,
including the Marlboro fire chief and the sheriff of
Windham County. These seemed eager to do their part,
but generally uncertain of what that part was.

No Eating, Please

The sheriff approached a Springfield couple opening a picnic lunch in their car. He had instructions that eating was not allowed just there, just then. Asked why, he produced several embarrassing answers all referring in some way to "security." Later he asked a group of youths to move from another area. "But what could we possibly do to Mr. Humphrey?" one of them asked. The sheriff pleaded a little in an apologetic way and then walked away, nonplused. Several more times he approached the group, but to no avail.

When Humphrey arrived just before 3 P.M., he found he was to have competition. Not only was the program to include pianist Rudolph Serkin playing in Schubert's "Trout" quintet, but cellist-conductor Pablo Casals was making a surprise visit to conduct Mozart's "Haffner" Symphony, and to the Marlboro audience this was at least as important as Humphrey's visit.

Applause

"Who just came in, Humphrey or Casals?" one woman whispered when the crowd stood and applauded upon the entrance of the vice-president.

All attention focused on the performing stage for the next hour, as Marlboro produced the best it had to offer. A sparkling "Sonata a quatro," for four strings written by Rossini when he was 12, was the opener.

The performance that followed of the famous Schubert piano quintet was televised by NBC, which now has on its tapes perhaps the best "Trout" ever recorded.

LAST ACT

At intermission, Humphrey was besieged by photographers and autograph seekers, but this was to be his last act before the spotlight shifted.

For Marlboro has its true heroes, and when Casals walked to the podium, the applause was longer than that for Humphrey earlier. A fast-paced, exhilarating half-hour later, the audience again saturated the air with bravos, and Casals took four calls to acknowledge them, only once bowing directly toward the vice-president in the third row.

When it was all over, Humphrey appeared with Serkin and walked several hundred yards to the motorcade that would take him to Serkin's nearby home for lunch. He was followed in his stroll by a good number of photographers.

CROWD WAITS

The Marlboro crowd, however, let Humphrey go, preferring to gather around the door and wait longer. When Humphrey had come out, all had been silent except the constant clicking of the cameras. But when Casals appeared, a slight man with a benevolent face, there were more cheers and applause.

The crowd surged with Pablo's car the length of the drive, and he waved repeatedly to his admirers. After the car drove out, the people discovered there was no more "security." Then someone noticed the vice-president also had gone.

SINKHOLE

A sinkhole has opened up
Right here in the center of my lawn,
About three feet across,
The sod folded raggedly
Around the edge, drooping
Into the depths. My wife
Will not go near it for fear of being
Dragged down to the dark space
From which you can just hear the gurgle
Of an old stone culvert
Which has concluded
That one hundred years of stalwart duty
Is enough.

If I were a real poet, sitting here
In my green Adirondack chair this
          perfect evening,
The bursting leaves luminous and still
In the late sun, I would
Write the yawning void
Beneath the green lawns of our lives
The stealthy collapse of foundations;
Write the hidden trickle of time
Down there in the culvert
Sluicing away any illusory
Slivers of happiness yet remaindered
To us.

Soon enough, I would write, the whole house
The very edifice of our ordered lives,
Must topple, any day now
And fall in,
Despite this sweet waft of lilac
On the breeze.

Instead, I write merely
That I bask in the late light
In the late spring,
The larger dog on my right
The little one on my left, both of them
Learning to eat carrots.

John Drysdale, 1905-2000

My father, John Drysdale, the third publisher of what is now
The Herald of Randolph, died on April 10, 2000. This is his obituary.

RANDOLPH—John Drysdale, who published the *White River Valley Herald* (now *The Herald of Randolph*) for 26 years and brought it into the modern age of offset printing, died Monday, April 10, 2000, of complications from pneumonia. He was 94 and had been in good health until his final illness.

He was born on Memorial Day, 1905 in the manufacturing city of North Adams, Mass. of Scottish immigrant parents, James and Jean (Monteath) Drysdale.

His father and, later in life, his mother both worked in the textile industry in North Adams.

After high school, John Drysdale worked a year for a North Adams clothier before enrolling at Brown University, from which he graduated in 1928. At Brown he was on the freshman diving team and was a member of the Flying Club.

After Brown, he enrolled in graduate studies in economics at Harvard University, but with the onset of the Depression, he was forced to drop out after one semester and go back to his job at the North Adams clothing store.

Somewhat later he offered to work his two-week vacation for free at the *Springfield Union*, the predominant newspaper in western Massachusetts, and quickly obtained a position as staff reporter.

During his years in Springfield, he met and married Eleanor Dickey, daughter of the newspaper's late editor. He was transferred to Boston to report from the state capitol and became knowledgeable about Massachusetts state politics, signing on eventually as political reporter for the *Boston Traveler*, a daily newspaper subsequently purchased by the *Boston Herald*.

In 1945, pursuing a lifelong dream of owning his own newspaper, he purchased *The Herald*, then known as the *White River Valley Herald*, from Luther B. Johnson, who had published it for 51 years. He built *The Herald* into a weekly newspaper with a statewide reputation for quality, and was active in town development projects, while his wife joined the school board and was instrumental in winning approval for construction of both the junior high and vocational schools.

In 1960, John Drysdale converted *The Herald* to the offset method of printing and production. Within the office that switch became known as "upset" rather than "offset," and he accomplished it two years before any other newspaper in Vermont. He was particularly pleased to be able to print clear photographs of people, especially children. The new printing method led directly to *The Herald*'s unique policy of printing baby pictures under the "I'm One!" heading.

In 1971, he sold *The Herald* to his son, the current publisher, but a planned retirement was interrupted by the untimely death of his wife 18 months later.

In 1975, he married a former college friend, Virginia Paine MacDaniel, and moved to her home in San Antonio, Texas, where he spent 20 wonderful years as stepfather and grandfather to her family of four sons and their wives, and children. They spent summers in his wife's childhood home in Abington, Connecticut, with frequent trips to Vermont.

None of his career accomplishments brought him more satisfaction than his successful marriages to two strong, independent, and lively women.

Virginia Drysdale died in 1995 and John returned to Randolph, to be closer to his family, eventually moving to the Joslyn House in Randolph and most recently to the Four Seasons Home in Northfield.

He was a longtime member of the Gifford Hospital board of directors, a board member of the White River Valley Development Corp., president of the Vermont Press Association, a life member of the Appalachian Mountain Club, and a member of the University Club and Rotary.

He was fond of hiking, swimming, and camping, especially in his beloved northern Berkshires. He continued to be informed about national and international issues well into his 90s.

He leaves three children, M. Dickey of Randolph, Isobel of Pueblo, Colo., and Ellen of Berlin; four grandchildren, Robin and James Drysdale and Jean and David Squires; and four stepsons, Sherman, Gibbs, Alfred, and

Putnam MacDaniel and their families in Texas and Seattle, Washington.

He was predeceased by a sister, Jean, in 1964.

A memorial service will be held at Bethany Church in Randolph at 2 P.M. on Friday, April 14, led by the Rev. Kathy Eddy.

Burial will be in a family plot in North Adams. The Day Funeral Home is in charge of arrangements.

Donations in lieu of flowers may be made to the Eleanor Dickey Drysdale Scholarship Fund at Randolph Union High School, which gives an award annually to the best writer in each senior class.

SNOWFALL

When the snow is falling, it is hard to believe that it will ever stop or, for that matter, that it ever began.

When the snow is truly falling, millions upon hopeless millions of snowflakes everywhere, on every side, closing off the sky above with their inexorable oncoming, it is as though it had always been snowing, as though the whole world were a place of snowing, unthinkable without snowing.

We entered that world again this week, that quiet muffled world of flakes. It is a world that draws itself about us, closer and closer as the snow falls faster. The wider world, its edges rounded and softened, disappears from our sight; the snow itself becomes the world: hypnotic, dancing, flickering with slight but enormous movement. Random but ordered, a snowfall looks like a brook sounds; it fills the sense but does not focus it; it is simply there, gently but overwhelmingly there. Everywhere.

Against that restless constancy of the snow, in the center of that collapsing, dimming world, the lights of home and hearth shine almost startlingly bright: warm cubes of yellow light. The clear-eyed living rooms and the ceaseless snowflakes regard each other through a glass pane, staking their boundaries. Inside, the house is full of air, transparent; outside, there seems no air at all, only the texture of the snow.

Now, the falling snow has obliterated the world entirely, folded it around us, wrapping us in a cocoon of motion and quiet, until we listen to our hearts. The snow will never end, and we accept that. It is a delicious and comfortable acceptance, a glad surrender.

But the unthinkable time comes after all, when one senses the snowfall is changing. The flakes fall more slowly; they fall doubly, then singly, idly. Space opens between them; the night air grows black with itself.

The storm is over.

In our homes, our own pupation, too, is over; the soft cocoon has unraveled around us and as morning breaks, we see it has fallen away altogether. Stretching our wings, we blink at the light, step into the snow, and glide out over the world, newborn.

BILL BURGESS

Bill Burgess was a great town manager.
I could see that the time I visited with him
Down at the landfill

And some contractor came up
And had every sort of thing to say
About every sort of thing and
None of it good. But Bill
Wouldn't answer a peep.

Not for the longest time.

He chewed on that big cigar and
Let the smoke circle above his head and he
Just laid his eyes on Mr. Contractor who
Raved and argued and maybe had time
To listen to himself a little bit. And then

In the slowest drawl imaginable Bill
Made one observation or another,
Something about grader mechanics
Or the lateness of the summer
And maybe a smidgen that was
Related to that contract—or maybe
Not. Nothing was resolved.

But when Mr. Contractor clambered
Back into his pickup, you could see
He was well-satisfied.

CHARLEY SPOONER:
A LIFE FROM ANOTHER TIME

*Published on March 10, 1988, this article won
the top reporting prize from the Vermont Press Association.*

BETHEL—Charles W. Spooner, 89, died February 13, 1988, at his residence on Spooner Road. He was born the youngest of 12 children in Bethel, on December 15, 1898, to Louis and Julia (Pecour) Spooner.

For many years, he operated the family farm on the Spooner Road and continued milking two cows. He loved animals and was the owner of several dogs.

That's all there was for a biography in *The Herald* when Charley Spooner died last month.

Indeed, that's about all anybody could say about Charley—if, that is, you wanted to talk about events, milestones in a life, achievements.

There weren't any to speak of.

Yet when Charley Spooner died, people who knew the name recognized that a void had been created that could not be described by the usual biographical data.

After all, not everybody has a road named for him. And a lot of people had heard tales about the man who lived at the very end of Spooner Road (the road joins Route 12 at Salter's Furniture south of Randolph).

Some had heard only of his eccentricities. Charley Spooner, for instance, possessed rocks which were valuable to him because he could discern sacred writings upon them, writings which were not apparent to others.

Spooner also had, as the biography stated, "several dogs."

In this case, "several" is an understatement, because for years there had seldom been fewer than ten. Any visitor or explorer who drove past the old farmhouse would be greeted by an alarming howling and barking and could be pardoned for the impression that there were dogs everywhere. The dogs were a considerable disincentive for anybody who might want to alight from his vehicle and find out more about their owner.

And yes, there was more to be learned about Charley Spooner. There was truth to the impression that the man who resided there in such splendid isolation had a story to tell.

Finding the truth about Charley Spooner, however, was hard. That's because the truth itself was a difficult truth, a truth so strange to modern eyes that it was hard to see and describe. Even those closest to him groped haltingly for words to explain why this man had made an impression on them, why his story was not only a strange one but a story of strength and importance, from which everyone might learn.

"'I've never spent a night off the farm,' that's what he always said," reminisced Stuart Osha one afternoon recently.

Osha and Joel Whitney, both young Randolph men, knew Spooner as well as anyone in recent years. Osha owns the next home down the road and believes in neighboring. Whitney met Spooner while still a youth, hunting in the area, and became a frequent visitor.

Whether it was literally true that Spooner never in 80 years slept off the farm property is not certain, but it might well have been, Osha and Whitney said. Spooner liked to tell of attending his brother's funeral in St. Albans, hurrying back to Spooner Road to keep his record intact.

"That was pretty important to him," said Whitney.

It is certain, at any rate, that he was born on the farm, had seen his parents die there, and that on February 13th, he himself died there.

He traveled very little. His father, before moving to Spooner Road, had built a house on Bear Hill in Brook-field, and Charley had been there at least once, in 1928.

"The amazing thing in talking to Charley," said Osha, "he would talk about this farm in Brookfield—like we would talk about a trip to California."

"Or he would talk to somebody from East Bethel, and he would say, 'I was there once.'"

In recent years, he left the farm less and less, perhaps only twice a year. "Why would I want to go anywhere? I like it here," he would argue.

"Here" was a scenic farm that had once been several hundred acres but which was forty-three acres at the time of Spooner's death. From those acres, Spooner had wrested enough to live.

A MAN AT 15

Being the youngest of 12 children, he had been only 15 when his father died and he took over the farm. With his mother he managed an average herd of about 40-50 head, 30 of which he milked by hand.

With his horses, he hauled lumber and pulp out of the forest. He loved animals and kept them well cared for.

He was no hermit. He drove a car, starting with a Model T in the 1930s and ending with a 1952 Ford which he drove (so slowly that a line of cars formed behind him) until the mid-60s. He bought one tractor about 1960.

But he never liked driving, and kept a soft spot in his heart for his horses: "He was all horses," is how Joel Whitney puts it.

He was a prodigious worker, as long as he could get around.

"I would hear that tractor going in the morning and not stop all day long," said Osha.

"He grew enough potatoes to feed the town of Randolph," chimed in Whitney.

Spooner didn't get about much, but that didn't mean he was ignorant about the world.

"The first mistake anybody would make was to take him for somebody who didn't know what was up," Osha related.

He never voted, but considered himself a Democrat and he read the papers to keep up on the mistakes of Republican officeholders.

Nor was he any fool when it came to negotiations. He liked to tell about the man who bought 200 acres from him and had the land surveyed. It turned out there were not really 200 acres, and the man came to ask him about it.

"Did you read your deed," asked Spooner, "where it says '200 acres more or less'? Well, you got less."

His sense of humor could have the same bite to it. He recalled a visitor who customarily left his wad of chewing tobacco on the windowsill. One day, Spooner replaced it with a concoction which included chicken droppings.

The visitor got awfully mad, but not at Spooner. He rushed down to Merusi's store to give Emil what-for for selling him bad tobacco.

The face Spooner turned toward the world was a hard one.

"He would pretend he didn't give a damn," Whitney said. But stories of his soft-heartedness got around anyway. There was the day he rescued one Emily Martin who had fallen while out getting wood. There was his continuing kindness toward Old Joe Silver, a dimly-remembered part of Randolph history who lived on the road to the dump. Spooner made it a point to drop by Joe's place, making fires for him, bringing him water, once pulling him out of the brook.

Mostly, though, he kept to himself and to the life he loved.

He Was It

It's that quality of fierce independence that today makes Stuart Osha and Joel Whitney shake their heads.

"He was it," said Whitney. "Independence, self-sufficiency."

"Money had no meaning to Charley. It was his life on the farm that counted."

"He didn't understand why I went in to work in an office every day," Osha said.

"He told me to give up my job and find a cabin somewhere," Whitney chipped in.

"One thing he was set on," said Osha. "He liked the old days best, the farming with horses. That was the way to live."

He paused, then explained further.

"Trying to see how far ahead you can get was not the point."

"This is what is lacking now," Osha reflected, struggling to present the strange power of this old man. Spooner's life, he said, represented a sort of satisfaction just with existing, rather than a struggle for constant advancement.

"Even when he was young he liked the old times."

It was natural then, that as he grew older, Spooner just continued doing the same things, only fewer of them. He sold off some of the land, and reduced his herd.

He kept busy. Just last summer he was still caring for five cows, and he milked at least one until a year ago. He cut wood. He kept working.

"His life…he did it all wrong," mused Osha, "if you listen to what they tell you to do today. He chewed tobacco, ate lots of fat, drank."

He talked to visitors, those who dared get past the dogs (which never bit anyone, Osha and Whitney said).

VISITING

"He said he didn't like visitors, but if you went there you'd better have your lunch with you," Whitney smiled. He himself loved to listen for hours to Charley Spooner's stories, some of which had to be taken with more than a grain of salt.

"He was a terrible guy to get away from," agreed Osha.

Spooner kept cider in the basement for special occasions—but most any visitor was occasion enough for him to "zing down to get a pitcher."

As he moved well into his 80s, he gave up enough of his independence to let his friends help him, but he didn't like it.

"It was an interesting experiment to try to get up his winter wood," Osha said. He remembered one fall when it became obvious that Spooner wouldn't be able to complete splitting some wood.

"One day we just up and split it and put it in for him," he said.

"But he complained about that wood all winter."

"Joel did more for him than anyone," Osha said appreciatively.

Charley Spooner died as independent as he had lived. Right up to the last week of his life he kept a cow and did his own chores.

The night before he died, Joel Whitney was up at his place a good deal of the night. He thought he had talked Spooner into seeing a doctor the next day and wanted the place spruced up.

"His mind was as sharp as a tack," he said. "He pointed to a piece of beech, which he wanted just so on the fire."

"It was just hours before he died."

The next day, Spooner changed his mind about the doctor. Osha, visiting a little later to transport him, found him dead in the chair in front of the fire.

Spooner's mother had died in the next room, and Charley had liked to tell about that night.

"I came in from chores to get supper ready, and I knew something was wrong," he had told his friends. "I knew she was dead."

It was in the middle of a snowstorm. Spooner had made his way to the foot of the hill to call for a snow-plow. When the response wasn't fast enough from Randolph, he called Montpelier and got a state plow to clear the road.

When his brothers and sisters arrived for the funeral, Charley had given them a piece of his mind for crying and carrying on.

"She had a good life, and who are you to wish her back just because you miss her," Charley Spooner had told them.

Joel Whitney: "I guess that's the way I feel about him."

Stuart Osha: "You can't have it any better."

WITHOUT SPARKY

After fifteen years with us
Sparky died just three days
after Christmas. Now it's July
And I walk out of the house
Shut the door
Cross the lawn
And disappear into the car
While the old house regards me
Through blank windows
Without a trace
Of regret.

CHRISTMAS PARTY
AT THE FREIGHT HOUSE

*For 13 years starting in the 1990s, the old wooden railroad
freight house in South Royalton housed a rousing jam session
of country and traditional music every Thursday evening,
often lasting for hours.*

It seemed an odd place for a Christmas party, this
long wooden building shoehorned in along the railroad
tracks. The floor was scattered with power equipment—
drills, saws, probably a lathe if I knew what a lathe
looked like. There was a gorgeous handmade wooden
bed at one end.

The walls were crowded with every kind of antique
tool, but also an African bust, a peace sign, notices pro-
claiming "Damaged Freight," and "No Hunting" and
"Private Crossing." A pair of ladies' high heel shoes
was sticking out of the ceiling.

An odd place for a Christmas party. But what a
party it was!

The date was Thursday, December 22, 2005 and the
place was the former railroad freighthouse in South
Royalton, which is now Freight House Woodworks,
where woodworker Randy Leavitt turns out his stunning creations by day.

By night, once a week, Leavitt hosts a jam session for
area musicians in the old Freight House, and at the end
of the year, they all get together for a Christmas party.

This particular evening, close to 75 people crowded into the Freight House, and all eyes were on Jim Abbott, though Jim didn't know it. Jim is one of the regulars at the Freight House, a big guy with shaved head and short beard and a perpetual smile on his face. He's always one of the first to welcome a newcomer, and he plays a mandolin, a stringed instrument that looks like a toy in his big hands.

This was to be Jim Abbott's night.

About a month earlier, Randy Leavitt had made a little speech to the Freight House musicians—a mixed bunch who typically play a dozen fiddles, almost as many guitars, with a sprinkling of mandolins, banjos, keyboards, pennywhistles, accordions, flutes, and even a cello.

In his speech, Randy disclosed that Jim's mandolin was on its last legs, and that Jim's Mandolin Fund at the Randolph National Bank had not been growing as he'd hoped it would.

"I just thought—maybe we can help him out," he said. He pledged that the contents of the Freight House jar, money that usually helps buy heat for the building, would instead be dedicated to a new mandolin for Jim Abbott. He hoped the group might be able to put $300 to $400 in the jar by Christmas to help with a second-hand mandolin.

It turned out that fundraising for a mandolin for Jim Abbott was the easiest thing in the world.

Abbott had grown up in South Royalton, attending school at the old building that is now part of Vermont Law School. Everybody knew him, and everybody liked him. It was impossible not to.

He had gotten interested in playing music during a year spent in Colorado—about the only time he's spent living away from central Vermont. When he came home, he found a mandolin in a friend's attic and the friend gave it to him, warning him that "it's a piece of crap." But it was good enough to learn chords on, and Jim was on his way with a new love that would become a big part of his life.

"I've had such a wonderful time with it," he exclaimed. He also discovered the Freight House jam sessions, and quickly became a regular.

"I love the feeling there," he said. "I love the acceptance...everybody's smiling. I just can't not go there every week."

The word about Jim Abbott's mandolin ran like wildfire through the South Royalton community.

"I started getting envelopes that I didn't even know who they were from," Randy Leavitt recalls. "They had notes in them as well as checks—really sweet stuff."

Predictably, some of the notes were addressed to the "Jimmy Fund."

Abbott had worked for eight years in maintenance at Vermont Law School, so the checks and notes started coming from the Law School, too, from the top administration on down.

By the time of the December 22nd Christmas Party, the jar on the Freight House table was full, and then some. Until 9 P.M. the evening reverberated with the usual sweet jigs and airs, with the addition of a Christmas round.

In a preview to the main event, folk singer Terry Diers made a presentation of a handsome "redneck cowgirl cello stand" he had made by hand for Suzanne Long, an organic farmer on Route 110 who is teaching him her instrument.

Then Randy Leavitt gave a speech, a Freight House speech about how a community can form a kind of dome over you, connecting people in manifold ways, and how Jim was part of so many little communities.

Then he brought out the jar.

A torrent of checks and bills poured out as Abbott looked on astonished, taken completely by surprise. The total came to about $1700.

Abbott mumbled some words of thanks, and his face went to war with itself, torn between his usual broad smile and the tears that threatened to well up.

Jim's assembled friends, 50 or more, responded with cheers and an outpouring of raucus jokes and insults.

Weeks later, Abbott still radiated a glow that warmed everyone near him.

"I'm just so touched," he said. "I really don't have the words for it."

He found an excellent second hand Rigel R-100 mandolin handmade by Rigel Instruments, a noted instrument-maker on Railroad Street in Cambridge, Vt., for just about $1700. Two weeks later, he brought it to the Freight House jam session. He finds that, like any new love, "it's been keeping me up late."

The next week, Jim's sister, Susan Fogleman of New Hampshire, showed up at the Freight House just to experience the sessions that she said "are the love of Jim's life."

"Thanks to everyone for making Jim the happiest guy on the planet this Christmas," she wrote in a letter. "We venture to guess that this was his best Christmas ever."

And not just the best Christmas for Jim Abbott, either.

"Whenever I think about those ten minutes," Randy Leavitt said, speaking of the December 22nd presentation, "it just gladdens my heart."

Lots of other hearts too, we venture to say.

THE AFFLICTION

The fact that my Boston son
Dropped his only key to the Dodge Spirit
Through a hole in his pocket,
Rendering useless an elderly
But perfectly serviceable sedan,
Is not funny.
The raw edge of panic in his voice
Could tell you that.

The fact that my Ithaca son
Does have a key to the Spirit but it's
Locked up in his Neon and
He can't find the key to the Neon:
That's not funny, either.

The fact that both sons' immediate progenitor,
As we speak, is breaking into
The Hide-a-Key Disguised as a Rock
In order to gain entrance
To his own office

There's nothing at all amusing
About that.
So why
Are you laughing, you?

Central Vermont Rallies
'Round Martha Pellerin

*Martha Pellerin was responsible in the 1980s and 90s
for a new appreciation for French Canadian music in Vermont,
reclaiming the music that had thrived in "kitchen junkets" in
French-Canadian homes. The wave of popularity directly
resulted in, among other things, Randolph's annual
New World Festival of Music and Dance.
When this article was written, Pellerin was in the last stages of
the cancer which would take her life, much too soon.
The article appeared in the Barre/Montpelier Times-Argus.*

Everybody knew in advance that Vermont's love for
Martha Pellerin couldn't be contained in a neat two-
hour concert. So nobody was surprised when Sunday
afternoon's extravaganza at the Barre Opera House ran
nearly four hours before the finale, when performers
and audience alike intertwined in a snake-like dance
around the seats and across the stage, a half-dozen
fiddlers keening a minor-key reel.

The concert, called "Vive la Rose," was a tribute to
Pellerin, who has worked tirelessly to revive the Franco-
American heritage in central Vermont—in particular, its
music. The Opera House was nearly filled with admirers;
proceeds benefited the Martha Pellerin Children's Trust
Fund.

What a glorious four hours they were! For an event
at a sad time—Pellerin is suffering from cancer—the
concert pulsed with joy, though it was a bittersweet joy.
A dozen performing groups donated their time and

others had to be turned away, according to Kevin Dunwoody of Brookfield, who with his wife Marie conceived and organized the event.

Perhaps the most poignant moment of a poignant afternoon came with just one person on stage. Storyteller Michel Parent, switching rapidly between English and French, told about his grandfather, who walked on crutches, having contracted polio as a youth. His zest for life, however, had made his handicap a kind of godsend for his young children, whom he allowed to ride on his crutches while he walked, swinging them back and forth with abandon.

"There are some people who forever change the way we look at life," the storyteller reflected. Then, turning directly toward Pellerin in the front row, he said softly, "Thank you, Martha."

Indeed, several American-born performers described their French-ness as having been felt as a handicap before Pellerin's enthusiasm transformed it into a treasured possession.

One after another they sang and played and sang and danced their thanks. The incomparable virtuosos of Manigance came together again just for the concert. Josee Vachon brought a talent for emceeing as well as singing with her smooth three-woman ensemble from Massachusetts. Jean Paul Loyer brought his insistent banjo, whose tunes lingered in the ear hours later. Pete Sutherland practically brought Louis Beaudoin himself back to life on stage with a masterly rendition of one of his fiddle favorites.

And accordionist and dance-master Benoit Bourque-Benoit brought pure joy in the little persons of the 40 members of Les Danse des Enfants. Schoolchildren, they danced with spirit and grace and commitment. They danced with brooms and adzes and sometimes with glasses of water on their heads.

At the end, it was the presence of Les Enfants on stage, as the dance-line snaked and fiddles shrieked and Benoit, big as a moose, stood grinning in the middle of it all—it was these happy youngsters who best reflected what Martha Pellerin taught, and what she has given to us all.

An Inconvenient Blizzard

Vermont's great Valentine's Day blizzard of 2007 came on the worst possible day of the week for *The Herald*.

Wednesday, as many of our readers know, is The Big Day—production day, the day in which Thursday morning's paper has to be completed and taken to the *Valley News* in West Lebanon for printing. Snowstorm or no snowstorm. Many businesses and offices, looking out the window at the appalling rate of accumulation, could make the quick decision that it was time to go home. But that was not an option at *The Herald*.

The blizzard also decided to arrive during a week when *The Herald's* editor and publisher was away on vacation. Horrors—a rudderless ship adrift on the sea of storms?

Not likely! Under the editorial leadership of Sandy Cooch and the production leadership of just about everybody, the decision was made to move full speed ahead, putting aside worries about how the staff would be able to get home. The second decision was to proceed as quickly as possible so that delivery of the completed pages to West Lebanon would be a physical possibility.

Sandy Cooch reports that the mood of cooperation and good spirit throughout the *Herald* offices made her job vastly easier. When staffers finished their regular jobs, they asked for another, until the whole job was done. The paper, a full 28 pages with full advertising support and great news and photos, was completed just before 2 P.M. instead of the usual 4:30 P.M.

Still there remained the pressing question: How were these precious 28 pages to be delivered to West Lebanon? Phone calls confirmed that the *Valley News* was still open for business and could print the paper if it got the pages. A glimpse out of doors, however, plus the broadcast warnings to stay off the road at all costs, argued strongly that this was one week when *The Herald* would have to be late. The decision was made not to attempt the trip.

But then there was a reconsideration. Photographer and writer Bob Eddy consulted a friend who was encouraging. He also took a look over his shoulder at the unbroken tradition of always publishing on time, and he decided to pack the pages into his all-wheel-drive Subaru and drive. There were times during the next hour that he thought he had made the wrong decision. The driving lane of Interstate 89 was passable, but visibility was terrible at the best of times. The worst of times came when tractor-trailer trucks roared by in the passing lane, which was covered a foot thick with powdery snow which ballooned everywhere as the trucks passed. The ensuing "white-out" was complete every time a truck passed, leaving other drivers totally unable to see where they were, where the road was, or how fast they were going. The terrifying experience was repeated several times.

Nevertheless, the delivery was made, and thanks to the *Valley News* crew, the bulk of the February 18, 2007 *Heralds* were at the White River Junction on Wednesday night as usual. The Randolph area papers and assorted store papers, usually delivered after printing on Wednesday night, were just slightly delayed until Thursday morning when our regular driver made the still-difficult trip back to West Leb to pick up those deliveries.

ON THE HOME FRONT

After these Wednesday night heroics, the *Herald* staff turned to the same problems that the rest of the Vermont world was experiencing. Copy editor Martha Slater of Rochester accepted an overnight invitation to stay with receptionist Kyle Southworth. Then she went home and, over the next three days, single-handedly shoveled her driveway and walk, and the church pastor's walk for good measure. Ad salesman Bob Martin tackled his long, windy Randolph Center driveway with his truck plow, then went to plow out a friend and became stuck for hours (a common story throughout the valley).

Bob Eddy overnighted with his mother in town, joined by his wife, Rev. Kathy Eddy, who skied four miles from their Braintree Hill home to visit with a family for pastoral care.

And where was the editor and publisher vacationing, you may ask?

He and wife Marjorie are cross country skiers, and they had traveled 600 miles to Gaspé Peninsula of Quebec, looking for some good fresh snow.

Right now, they're feeling pretty grateful. Thanks, everyone!

148

A Lesson from Virginia

During a workshop for newspaper editors in Virginia in 1990,
the press sessions took a back seat to events in Virginia
and the treasured monuments of our national capital.

The Commonwealth of Virginia showed a thing or two to one Vermont Yankee last week.

It's easy for a New Englander to feel superior as he crosses the Mason-Dixon Line and heads into the South. After all, the North won the war.

But last Saturday, January 13, 1990, as we arrived in Virginia for a week's sojourn, the Old Dominion did something that no northern state has ever done: It swore into office a black governor. Lawrence Douglas Wilder became the first black man to be elected governor anywhere in this country.

As 30,000 watched in person and millions tuned in on television, Wilder took the oath of office, standing on a raised dais in Capitol Square in Richmond.

Richmond, Virginia. The capital of the Confederate States of America. The moment teemed with symbols; the heart leapt.

And what did L. Douglas Wilder choose to say on this momentous occasion?

It would have seemed natural to quote the Rev. Martin Luther King, Jr., whose birthday was two days later. But Wilder chose older words to speak. Deliberately, he chose the words of a fellow Virginian, Thomas Jefferson.

"We hold these truths to be self-evident," he intoned, *"that all men are created equal, that all are endowed by their creator with certain inalienable rights…"*

As he spoke them, these words—these 214-year-old words—seemed to explode out of history, thundering down through the years like cannon shots to the present. Did Jefferson, as he wrote them, have any inkling of the power flowing from his pen, of the years those phrases would span so effortlessly?

"I feel like I'm here on behalf of five generations of my family," Douglas Wilder said, his face beaming with undisguised joy. "I'm looking at things my grandmother and great grandmother scarcely dreamed of."

Across the Potomac, in the District of Columbia, are other words, words which recall Jefferson's but which testify to the terrible deeds which history required to give full meaning to his vision. Engraved in stone on the greatest of our national monuments it is written, "Four score and seven years ago, our forefathers brought forth upon this continent a new nation, conceived in liberty and dedicated to the proposition that all men are created equal. Now we are engaged in a great civil war, testing whether that nation or any nation so conceived and so dedicated, can long endure."

Mighty words, mighty deeds, so that the visiting Northerner feels humbled. And just as these words and deeds could not be contained in a single century of

American history, so they could not be contained either by the boundaries of the continent.

"Democracy," the students wrote on the walls in China earlier this year. "Democracy," the shout resounded in dozens of tongues and accents this fall and winter in Poland, in Germany, in Czechoslovakia, in Bulgaria, in Romania, in Yugoslavia, in Russia herself.

On the streets of Berlin, just before the Wall came down, the distinguished lineage of this great idea—from Jefferson, through Lincoln, through the Civil Rights struggles of this century—found touching expression: The song they were singing was in English, and the words were, "We shall overcome ..."

Through the centuries, Jefferson's words have rolled, throughout the world they have spread. In Virginia last week we felt privileged to witness such a potent reminder of them, and to remember what a seed was sown in American soil two centuries ago. And when we crossed the river to Washington, it didn't escape our notice that in this nation's capital, the monuments stand, not in tribute to wealth or empire, but to words and ideas.

Crossing into Washington, also, one was aware of the unfinished business of the American revolution. There was little sign of it among the national monuments, but this is one of the nation's most troubled cities, in which hundreds of thousands live in poverty-stricken and drug-ridden slums.

The great words of the past are little consolation to those trapped in such an environment, where freedom is illusory and equality is an invitation to submit to the lowest common denominator.

There are words for these people, too, spoken by Dr. King and engraved on a monument to him:

"No, we are not satisfied. And we shall not be satisfied until justice rolls down like waters, and righteousness like a rolling stream."

We hold these truths to be self-evident,
that all men are created equal.

"JUDEVINE:"
CONTROVERSIAL, CAPTIVATING

*Published October 2, 1986, this review won the
1986 Donoghue Award for arts criticism
from the Vermont Press Association.*

It took an Act of Congress for Robert Penn Warren
to be named national poet laureate last week, but in
Vermont, David Budbill won the post by acclamation.

Budbill's poem-play "Judevine" completed a triumphant
tour of Vermont Sunday at the Barre Opera House, a
tour which saw the play banned at Woodstock High
School but enthusiastically received by a crowd of 450
in the hardscrabble town of Hardwick, a tour which
drew big crowds wherever it appeared.

Thanks to an impeccable and affecting performance
by the Vermont Repertory Theater of Winooski, Budbill's three books of Vermont poetry came alive before
the wide audience the work deserves. The play, and the
poetry, achieved that rare phenomenon, acclaim from
the critics along with appreciation from the people.

I term "Judevine" a poem-play because it is not quite
a play; it's just a step removed from a poetry reading.
But what joy to see an audience of 400 weeping and
laughing and squirming at a poetry reading! And what
satisfaction to hear a dramatic presentation in which
each word is so well considered, each thought so cleanly
limned, each line so deeply true—a presentation, in
short, in which the actors speak poetry.

Truth is what got David Budbill into trouble—at first with his neighbors and then with a school principal. Reportedly some of his hometown folk in Wolcott didn't appreciate the first published portraits of Judevine, a town described as the "ugliest town in Northern Vermont—except maybe East Judevine." And the principal at Woodstock High School feared that some parents wouldn't appreciate some of the language in "Judevine," language which is sometimes thoroughly profane but which rings true, coming from the lips of its characters.

The success of "Judevine" is a tribute to the power of truth, affiring that when audiences see and hear the truth, they will recognize it, and respond to it.

Seeing "Judevine" for the audience, was much like wandering through one's own town in a dream, shaken to recognition by a joke here, a phrase there, a situation, an irony. The difference between Judevine and any real town—Wolcott, for instance—is that in Judevine the characters speak, although roughly and comfortably, with precision and grace.

REPERTORY THEATER

The success of this dramatic presentation is due not only to David Budbill and his poetry, however. The performance by the Vermont Repertory Theater was seamless and inspired. The voices, in particular, were wonderful. The members of the company did not have to do much Acting, but they did a wonderful job in dramatizing each poem. They had listened carefully to

154

the music of the words, they had responded to the characters, and their technical prowess was unquestionable.

It is also to the credit of the Repertory Theater and its founder and director, Robert Ringer, that "Judevine" came to the stage at all. Budbill made the stage adaptation especially at the request of Ringer (although an earlier stage version had been produced at Princeton University).

Ringer related that when the play opened last January, it was scheduled for three weeks performance in Winooski, the group's home. So popular was it that the run had to be extended another week. The touring performance started with another packed run in Winooski and proceeded to Henniker, N.H., and Mill River High School, Woodstock, Hardwick, St. Johnsbury and finally Barre.

What a fine and encouraging combination: a Vermont writer writing about Vermont, a Vermont theater with a Vermont director, putting poetry on the stage for hungry Vermont audiences!

An Impresario of Talk

The following was an editorial published at the death of Tom Winship, nationally known, award-winning Editor of the Boston Globe. Winship often referred to The Herald (in our presence, at least) as his "second-favorite newspaper."

One of the giants of the intellectual history of Boston was Dr. Oliver Wendell Holmes, the father of the Supreme Court Justice. Dr. Holmes was an eminent man of science, but his most famous role was as self-described "Autocrat of the Breakfast Table." The essays he published under that name described conversations, full of inquiry and wit, ranging throughout the worlds of politics, science, and society, over which Dr. Holmes presided.

That great Boston tradition of high-minded talk, spiced with humor and insatiable curiosity, was a legacy bequeathed to Randolph friends by Tom Winship, the fabled editor of the Boston Globe who died last Thursday. For 30 years, Winship maintained a second home on a beautiful south-facing farm high above East Randolph; and when he was visiting—which was often—he loved nothing better than presiding at table.

Tom Winship, however, was no autocrat, and dinner was his choice venue, not breakfast. Rather than an autocrat of the breakfast table, he became for his Randolph friends a sort of Democrat of the Dinner Table, a genial impresario of good food and good talk.

No topic was too large or too local to escape his lively interest. He drew out businessmen about business, farmers about farming, historians about history, artists about their art. Nor was any guest allowed to fade into the woodwork: Tom Winship was sure that each had a story to tell, a perspective to illumine, and he made sure their contribution was heard. Just when conversation was flagging, he popped another Big Question, and all had to have their say.

For his guests, it was a little hard to connect this genial, informal host to the grandeur of his reputation in Boston and in journalism, the man who turned a major metropolitan newspaper upside down, collected Pulitzers as if they were trinkets, and was universally recognized as one of a handful of the best editors in the country.

But as we read the brimming obituaries and columns in the *Globe*, the *New York Times*, and elsewhere, we recognized the qualities we had seen over the dinner table. This same curiosity about everything, this same enjoyment of people of every stripe, especially people younger than he was, this same drive to find a shape for current events—with these qualities he had led his newsroom to become a lively, committed place, swarming with his young "tigers," all energized by his inquiry and his faith in them.

Winship also brought to Vermont the activist persuasion that animated him as an editor—the simple drive to make things better. Always, he was trying to figure out ways for farmers to succeed—and he protected 400 acres of his own land from commercial development as his own contribution. He had a special interest, too in Randolph's struggles to keep its downtown viable after the fires of the early 1990s.

So entirely without pretense was Tom Winship that one never felt he was conferring conspicuous favors on this little town through his presence. He was, though. In the long tradition of Boston sages and patriots, he connected us to the larger world, to philosophic inquiry into great questions, all leavened by his infectious love of life. Grateful we are indeed for his sojourn amongst us.

EARLY IN THE EVENING

Early in the evening
I remove myself from the house
And take refuge on the porch
Where the cicadas are screaming.
I do not have to ask them
To repeat themselves—
Just one more time, for old dad
To hear it right, or almost right.

So kindly are those
Around the table inside,
Always, always making allowances even
As it must seem the old lights
Are growing dim.
And of course, they are right.
Every day I grow
More stupid:
Missing This altogether
Catching only part of That,
Misconstruing almost everything.
My once-proud arsenal of understanding
Quietly depleting.

America in Italy

*The Herald's editor, with his wife Marjorie,
returned Sunday from a two-week trip to Italy.
The trip was courtesy of the Randolph Singers,
who in December 1991 presented him with a European trip
in thanks for 20 years as their volunteer conductor.*

SPOLETO, ITALY—In Europe, one becomes accustomed
to looking at people and guessing where they live. Surrounded here by the people of the Mediterranean—dark
and handsome, fine of feature—one is almost taken aback
at seeing a group of fair, tall, and muscular Germans,
or long-legged Scandinavians. There's an undeniable
feeling of Otherness about them: They are people from
Across the Mountains, people from the Northern seas.
The differences, and the awareness of difference, are
part of the richness of Europe, part also, or course, of
its tragedies.

Spoleto itself is about as Italian as one can get, a
jumble of three-story homes and stores on an Umbrian
hillside, crowded inside its protective wall, climbing
building-upon-building via crooked lanes up the hill to
the crown of its castle, and just below the castle, to the
cathedral. Here during July is held one of the world's
best-known music festivals, the Festival of Two Worlds,
conceived by the Italian composer Gian Carlo Menotti
with concerts both in Spoleto, Italy, and in Charleston,
South Carolina.

And here to the Spoleto festival, a week ago Sunday, came an American chorus, the Westminister Choir of Princeton, New Jersey, to sing a program of choral and orchestral music at the 900-year-old cathedral. Italians packed the church to hear them, taking every seat in the nave and filling as well the choir stalls and the aisles.

Seated among the Italians were we, two Americans from Vermont, conscious that a modicum of national pride was on the line as the group from New Jersey ushered forth to sing.

And what a funny looking group of people they were! After just a week in Italy, surrounded by a certain physical type of people, a certain impeccable way of dressing, these Americans seemed almost bizarre in their diversity. There were great tall ones, little short ones, overweight ones, slender ones, people with great gangling awkwardness, people who were kind of square shaped. And there were colors of face and hair: from black to the blondest of blond, with every kind of swarthy and tan mixed in. In particular we noted the advent of a tall young man, with a pasty coloring, a slump, and a pony tail (the only one we saw in Italy). Next to him was likely a Jewish youth, fully a foot shorter, plump with tightly curled hair and a dark complexion. What an odd couple!

Finally all had filed in. They stood there, in uneven rows, facing their conductor, a genial sort of man with a sandy complexion and a certain naïve openness of feature that reminded one a little of Bill Clinton. What could this conductor do with this group of oddities?

As soon as the music started, there was no need to ask. The 400-year-old strains of a motet by William Byrd (English, probably raw-boned and awkward featured) spread through the cathedral, swelling and dying away into its high spaces. The voices from the 60 unequal throats mingled in the ether, blending, achieving a thrilling purity. The 60 voices became one and so, in an instant, did the faces and bodies with all their assorted shapes and sizes. No longer was this a motley group of individuals but a choir, a choir capable of a single expression, a single wish, a single hope for beauty.

From the Byrd motet, the choir progressed to Schubert, to a modern American work, and then to the monumental "Dona Nobis Pacem" which closes Bach's B-minor Mass. The packed cathedral responded with an enormous ovation, and the Americans sang the Bach again. The words mean "Give Us Peace," repeated over and over again, surging through the ancient church, the message as urgent and the music as powerful as when it was written 250 years ago. We caught a glimpse of the tall youth in the pony tail and his short neighbor. Both were singing fully and completely, eyes aglow, delirious with high delight. Again the audience roared and the two young men began grinning, responding with unforced pleasure to the tumult of approval as well as the musical peak they had just reached together. It felt good to be an American that day.

It wasn't until a little later that we realized what the day was. It was the Fourth of July. And it seemed to us then, and seems now, that the great American experiment had been played out before our very eyes. The peoples of many lands had assembled together, in all their diversity. The differences had not disappeared, but for two hours, they had been subsumed; the individuals had become one choir in the service of higher ideals and art.

It was a Fourth of July to remember.

A Lady Who Will Be Missed

A stone marker in memory of Randolph's Jean Montgomery,
who died in 1988, can still perhaps be found in a secluded
section of beach on the Scottish island of Iona,
placed there by a troupe of Randolph musicians
as their thanks for her years of guidance and friendship.

Jean Brigham Montgomery died last week, and Randolph is the poorer for her passing.

Jean had a prodigious musical talent. When she sat before the piano, she was able to play at sight music that most pianists would want to practice for a month. Whether it was a classical piece, a Rodgers & Hammerstein score, or a Gilbert & Sullivan romp, you could just put it onto the piano, and Jean would play it.

Never a problem, either, were complicated score reductions, in which the piano part is not written out but must be deduced by reading four or six musical lines, written independently on the score, one above another.

Many was the time that I, as director of the Randolph Singers, handed her such a score just as we were about to sing it, apologizing for not getting it to her to practice. Jean would make a face. Then she would play it.

A lot of people have talent, though. What was remarkable about Jean Montgomery is how she used hers.

Apparently it never occurred to Jean that she might hoard her music, saving it for special occasions or using it to promote a personal career. The music which came so easily to her she bestowed just as easily on others.

She loved to play, at any occasion, and seemed determined that this gift of hers, which seemed to make people happy, should be used as often as possible to do just that.

Nor did her talent need a formal occasion to call it forth. At any gathering of musical folk, it would take a mere suggestion about singing and Jean would be at the piano, playing. If there was printed music, fine. If not, fine too; Jean would play musical numbers out of her head. If you didn't like it one key, she would play it in a different one, without skipping a beat.

She played at home, or in other people's homes. She played in church, she played in schools. She taught dozens of youngsters, and she taught always the joy of music, as well as the technique. She was one of those who proposed the creation of the Randolph Singers in its present form, and she was the crucial element in its success. The effortlessness with which she played difficult passages, her patience in repeating them again and again, her willingness to be always there for special rehearsals, her happy satisfaction in seeing musical growth: these qualities enabled a musical organization to be created where nothing had been before. She was an extra set of ears for the director, detecting a wayward vocal line and emphasizing it on the piano. And for all this, she never asked for credit, never asked for a penny in payment.

Jean had a famous ability to accompany soloists who sometimes forgot their music or who sometimes sang a part a little differently than it was written, a common hazard in dealing with amateur musicians. No matter what the soloists sang or played, whether they left out a note or a line or whatever, Jean would be with them, guiding them through to the end of the piece.

In the past 20 years, Randolph has acquired a state-wide reputation both as a center of cultural achievement and a place with robust community spirit.

If anybody has nurtured that achievement and that spirit over the years, it has been Jean Montgomery.

Sunny and Seventy-Eight

Sunny and 78 degrees,
The car radio announces,
And even the long-distance haulers
Forsake the cloister of their
King cabs.

Down go the windows huge
Arms poke into the
70 m.p.h. airstream it
Whips their hair
Curls lightly behind their necks
In a caress,
Slips early summer fingers
Into their T-shirts.

Upstream of the White River bridge on I-89
A man and a boy
Rods arching towards the rapids,
Have waded well into
The stream they stand
Waist-deep
In diamonds.

Exactly then, a swallowtail
Dives through the window into
My own car,
Its moist touch against my neck mute
Assurance of a swift ending.
It lies beside me on the seat,
Wings spread,
Without a flaw.

BEST AND FAVORITE VERMONT PLACES

These pieces, published in The Herald on November 16, 2005, were solicited from writers by Tom Slayton for Vermont Life. Five of the eight sketches here were published in the magazine.

RIVER SWIMMING

Just north of South Royalton, marked by a five-car pull-off on Route 14, the White River creates its own water park. At the edge, flat rocks line the shallows, suitable for the very young and their moms and dads, while farther out, a lively current sweeps the daring ones downstream between boulders, speedily among riffles, and into a huge river pool, nearly a quarter acre in extent and 20 feet deep, swirling with water that is fresh and fragrant, unlike any lake or backyard pool you ever swam in. A ledge protrudes into the pool, a perfect spot for the teenagers to laze, and providing a nice 10-foot jump into the depths. On summer weekends, kayaks and tubes shoot the rapids into the pool, their occupants cheering lustily.

Before they discovered high-rock diving, this was our sons' favorite place in the whole world.

(Note: Tropical Storm Irene changed the configuration of the river park to some extent. It's still a good swimming hole, but not the perfect one it was.)

THE FALL LINE

The Fall Line at Mad River Glen Ski Area is one of just a few ski trails in Vermont that you have to climb up to. That 20 vertical feet of sidestepping above the famous single chairlift constitutes a rite of passage, a toll payment that admits you to the most beautiful ski trail in Vermont.

Even before you start down, you're enchanted by the wandering, narrow passageways between snow-laden spruces that can lead to a glimpse of Lake Champlain. There's a sense of having entered a sort of throne room for the privileged skier. That sense is of course heightened by the slight knot in your stomach, as you contemplate the gladed steeps beyond. This is the realm of the sublime, where beauty and danger dwell together. The Fall Line has admitted you to its magic kingdom, but now you have to get down the mountain all by yourself.

4-H Barns at the World's Fair

Of course the Tunbridge World's Fair belongs in any listing of best and favorite places—more specifically the 4-H barns down near the First Branch of the White River. There on a Saturday morning, youngsters prepare their calves for show among the white clapboard barns.

These eager and attentive ten- and twelve-year-olds, boys and girls alike, neglect nothing as their brushes caress the flanks, thighs, ankles and necks of their soft-eyed prizes. Parents, and brothers and sisters, offer advice. In the air lingers a timeless caring—the youngsters for the beasts they have nurtured for months, the beaming parents for their industrious children, and—oddly—the

Tunbridge World's Fair itself for this intimate rural ceremony it has fostered now for 134 years.

Watch closely, watch deeply; and when you turn away, your heart will be singing.

SILVER LAKE

Lake Dunmore in Addison County is beauty enough, overlooked as it is by lordly Mount Moosalamoo, but an even rarer jewel hangs in its tiara 700 vertical feet higher. Dropped into a declivity in the Green Mountain National Forest, mile-long Silver Lake offers a convincing illusion of solitude, even though it's only a mile by gentle uphill trail from popular Branbury State Park. Ringed by beach rock and verdant hills on all sides, its waters offer pure (and often chilly) refreshment to day hikers and the handful of families and camp groups who visit the Spartan lakeside campsites. It seems a world apart.

As it happens, Silver Lake is also haunted by history, especially the specter of one Frank Chandler, who for thirty years ran a sort of evangelical Chautauqua in his hotel on its shores. He required that his guests leave their pipes in an accumulating pile at the door as a sign of their personal, though perhaps temporary, defiance of Satan.

CHAMBER MUSIC AT CHANDLER MUSIC HALL

For those who love it, chamber music is the very essence of classical music—two violins, a viola and a cello and maybe a piano or flute, confiding the most intimate impulses of the great composers, which the symphony or opera are sometimes too grandiose to fathom.

And if there is a better place anywhere to hear chamber music than in 99-year-old Chandler Music Hall on Main Street in Randolph, I don't know where it is. The wood-and-plaster resonance of the stenciled hall, the high pressed-tin ceiling, the dimensions that are at once modestly grand and comfortably snug, all ensure that music here speaks warmly and directly to the listeners; the players themselves seem close enough to touch. The privilege is palpable.

Note: Every August for 13 years, Chandler Music Hall (which turned 100 in 2007) has hosted the two-week-long Central Vermont Chamber Music Festival; throughout the year the Hall's management continues a notable commitment to this commercially fragile musical form.

MAPLE RIDGE

The hiker on many Vermont trails finds himself navigating a tunnel of trees—it's all very pretty but a little lacking in adventure. A notable exception is the climb up Mt. Mansfield via the Maple Ridge Trail from Underhill State Park.

After a level mile, the trail begins a gazelle-like ascent of Maple Ridge itself. Steep (sometimes a little scary) ledge climbs lead to the top of one rocky knoll after another, each with its own spectacular view west and north, each offering amongst the fragrant bushes a few comfortable rocks that urge you to sit a minute, relax, take a load off, nibble some Fig Newtons. It's an invitation you should accept—several times if you want. What's the rush?

Unlike most Mansfield trails, Maple ridge is lightly traveled, and it leads to the very best Mansfield summit—the Forehead, spacious and bare and usually deserted. From there it is an easy stroll to the more populated Nose and Chin—or you can just turn around and enjoy Maple Ridge on the way down.

VERMONT HISTORY EXPO

For a quintessential Vermont celebration, it's hard to beat the Vermont History Expo, held every June since 2001 on the grounds of the Tunbridge World's Fair. There are many activities—entertainment, musketry, geneologies, historic impersonations—but the true core of the Expo can be found in the booths set up by 100 local history societies to share with you, breathlessly, what happened, once upon a time, in their towns.

Here is history as it ought to be told, far from the authoritative and authoritarian explanations that sternly fill our history books. This is history with the STORY writ large, an exultant, anarchic telling of bits and pieces of interesting stuff, stories of men and women who illuminated a span of years with their energy or eccentricities, or stories of violent spasms of nature against which the character of a people were occasionally measured.

And what storytellers! Visitors need merely to lift an eyebrow in curiosity to find an eager explainer near at hand, expounding on the topic in question, full of details and pleasure, telling the story.

The setting, too, is perfect. The Tunbridge Fairgrounds is a history expo all to itself, tucked into one of the most lovely valleys in all of Vermont, where Main Street looks virtually the same as it did 100 years ago.

MEDICAL MIRACLES IN ST. ALBANS

The St. Albans Historical Museum is a dandy place in all respects, but all else pales next to what you will find when you climb to the second floor and enter the Northwest Room. It's dedicated to the history of medicine and there, side-by-side, you will find two of the most grotesque, vivid, fascinating and historically important exhibits you will ever see.

One is Phineas Gage with a Five-Foot Iron Rod in his Head. The other is Mr. St. Martin with a Hole in his Stomach .

Definitely, bring the kids. This is history and science taught with an "Oh my goodness" immediacy, as the life-size models draw the viewer in to succinct explanations of two extraordinary medical stories, both of which resulted in breakthroughs in medical knowledge. Gage was said to have lost his moral sense after the accident, and his case led to early studies of the brain.

Mr. St. Martin's accident left him with a skin flap over his stomach that for years allowed direct inspection of what was going on in there. It's fascinating stuff, and sharing a room with these two gentlemen will stay with you for a long time.

Yesterday I Heard You Sing

Dedicated to Marjorie Balgooyen Drysdale

Yesterday I heard you sing again
As you sang in the sweet blossom of your youth
A heart-song from your perfect lips, like a
            holy garment
Straight from Beauty's treasure
Spilled into a universe which had
Never heard it before, not just so.

What if your name this time was Kate, or Jennifer
Or another of all those who spill
From college gates when they turn 21?
What if this time I felt you warm beside me,
            equally entranced
A grateful listener, not bestower of the gift?

And what if 30 years have fled since first you sang?

That voice we heard yesterday, yes, yes, was yours,
Again as then in Handel's silver shout—
"O sing! O sing unto the Lord"—
The song a prelude to a thousand more
Chanson and lied, a lifetime's torrent,
Surging through memories and dreams,
Collecting in the corners of the rooms.

Of late the songs are changed somewhat
With less of light and more of measure—
Less of Handel, more of Brahms—
Seasoned in the knowing sauce of time
But still now ringing forth once more
More beautiful, more moving than before.

And so I hoped while listening yesterday
That this you, this very Kate, herself
Might sing the years as full with song
As years have taught us years can hold.

I hoped she might return to us some day,
To Beauty still in beauteous thrall,
And singing Brahms.

ABOUT THE AUTHOR

At the age of six months,
M. Dickey (Dick) Drysdale
moved with his family to
Randolph, Vermont from
Concord, Massachusetts, a
fact which makes it impossible
for him to claim that he is a
Vermonter despite having
lived in the Green Mountain
State for most of his 70 years.

For almost 45 of those years he was the editor and
publisher of the 140-year-old *Herald of Randolph* (for-
merly the *White River Valley Herald*), following in the
footsteps of his father, who was publisher for 26 years.
The Herald, which circulates in 16 towns in rural central
Vermont, has consistently won awards from the Vermont
Press Association and the International Society of
Weekly Newspaper Editors for its photography and
writing, including editorial writing.

A continuing interest of the author has been Vermont's
cultural scene, and he won the Press Association's first
John Donoghue Award for writing on cultural topics.
He conducted the Randolph Singers, an accomplished
community chorus, for 25 years, and his wife Marjorie
Drysdale is also a choral conductor (leading "Sounding
Joy" for 27 years) as well as one of Vermont's premier
soprano soloists. Marjorie and Dick have two sons,

Robin, of Brooklyn, New York, and James, of Boise, Idaho.

In June of 2015, Drysdale sold *The Herald*, in which most of the articles in this book were originally published. Despite the accident of his birth, he hopes that his love for Vermont shines through these pages.

Made in the USA
Las Vegas, NV
29 December 2020